Bowling

Fifth Edition

Richard T. Mackey
Miami University
Oxford, Ohio

Mayfield Publishing Company
Mountain View, California
London • Toronto

Library of Congress Cataloging-in-Publication Data

Mackey, Richard Thomas.
Bowling / Richard T. Mackey. --5th ed.
p. cm.
Includes index.
ISBN 1–55934–161–0
1. Bowling. I. Title.
GV903.M22 1992
794.6--dc20 92-12893
CIP

Manufactured in the United States of America
10 9 8 7 6 5 4 3 2 1

Mayfield Publishing Company
1240 Villa Street
Mountain View, California 94041

Sponsoring editor, Erin Mulligan; production editor, Lynn Rabin Bauer; manuscript editor, Joanne McClintock; associate designer, Jean Mailander; manufacturing manager, Martha Branch; text designer, Elaine Wang; cover illustrator, Pauline Phung. The text was set in 11/12.5 Garamond and printed on 50# White Opaque by Malloy Lithographing.

Contents

Preface

I have been very pleased with the success of the past four editions of my bowling text. Since 1967, *Bowling* has been the most straightforward bowling fundamentals text available. Its condensed style and step-by-step approach have made it, for many, a bowling class necessity. The continued positive response to the text has inspired me to make this fifth edition a better resource that will help your students learn and enjoy the lifetime sport of bowling.

The new edition has been updated and revised to better serve your needs and the needs of your students. The most unique feature of the text continues to be its increased emphasis on learning bowling through audio-visual cues. The text facilitates your students' ability to recognize and teach themselves proper bowling techniques using audio-visual cues and mental imagery. The combination of these cues and the clear and accurate illustration program will help your students become their own teachers. This edition contains even more on imagery and the mental aspects of the game.

The fifth edition is full of other useful features that will help your students become better bowlers. Some have been retained from previous editions, and others are exciting new additions. Complete chapters on bowling terms, etiquette, and scoring invite students to learn the background information they need to participate fully in the sport. Chapter 2, on the history of bowling, has been updated and expanded to include lists of important milestones, records, and facts. If your students roll a few gutter balls they won't feel so bad when they learn that the record for "Most Consecutive Gutter Balls" is nineteen. The material on conditioning and warm-up for bowlers in Chapter 5 will help your students bowl injury-free. Chapter 7, "Common Faults and How to Correct Them," anticipates and answers the questions of beginning bowlers. An entire chapter on improving your score through spot bowling (Chapter 8) and the useful tear-out reference sheets on spot bowling (in the back of the book) are retained in this edition. Sample test questions with answers (in the Appendix) allow your students to check their progress and help you prepare testing material.

I would like to thank the following reviewers for their valuable suggestions: Douglas Rogers, Brevard College; Judson B. Harris, Jr., Jacksonville University; Elvin R. King, Cedarville College; and Jeffrey R. Mallas, Pennsylvania State University.

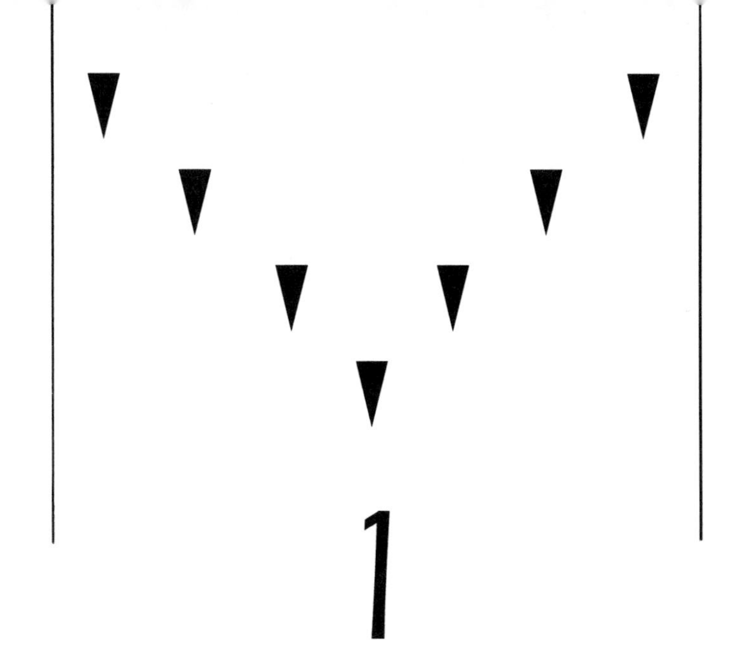

1

Your Approach to Bowling

What do you need to enjoy bowling? At the rate new bowlers are joining the devotees, a place to bowl might seem to be the prime necessity for bowling fun these days. It is a fact, however, that people feel satisfied when they do things with a degree of success. And what are the ingredients of successful bowling—the things that increase your enjoyment? Certainly your attitude toward the sport is important. Bowling is basically a game of finesse rather than power. Hurling the ball with tremendous speed and seeing the pins scatter can be a pleasure, but the satisfaction of consistently good performance comes with controlled speed. Although you can see much variation in the styles of top-notch bowlers, certain similarities will also be evident. Good bowlers are smooth bowlers, and they have a flowing motion as they approach the foul line and deliver the ball. Accomplished bowlers also have the good balance essential to outstanding performance. Besides the physical or mechanical aspects of the skill, there is the mental side of bowling. Poise and confidence based upon sound techniques are important. The development of these factors will increase your own enjoyment of America's number one indoor sport.

May this book contribute to both your bowling skill and your pleasure.

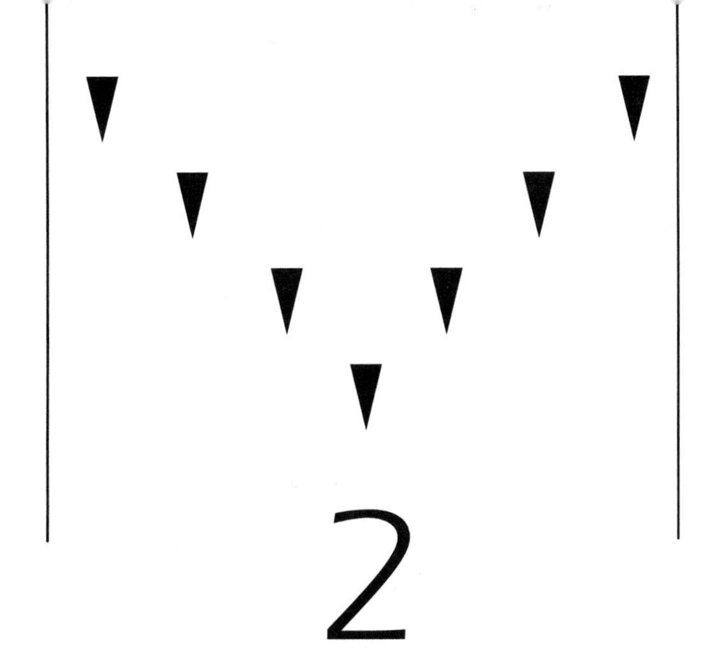

2

A Brief History of Bowling

The urge to throw a stone or a similar pellet at an object is basic to the play habits of people throughout the world, so it is not surprising to find the historical accounts of bowling going back seven thousand years. The Egyptians played a game similar to modern tenpins in 5200 B.C. According to some historians, bowling was introduced into Europe in 50 B.C. via the Italian game that has come to be known as *boccie*. And no history of the sport would be complete without mentioning the contribution of Wilhelm Pehle, a member of the German Bowling Society and Berlin Bowling Club. Pehle was a great student of the game. His book, *Bowling,* written in the nineteenth century, indicated that religion and bowling were closely associated as far back as the fourth century A.D. At that time bowling or *kegeling* was done in the cathedrals as a religious ceremony. The parishioners were asked to place their pins or *kegels* at the end of the cloister and then were given a round stone called a *heide* 'heathen'. If the *kegler* was successful in knocking over his pin, this indicated a clean and pure life. Failure to knock over the pin called for stricter adherence to church rules and regulations.

As time went on, changes in equipment and rules took place: Specially shaped pins were developed; small stones were replaced by larger ones; wooden balls were eventually substituted for stones. The game lost its religious significance, but it continued to be played by the upper class of laymen rather than by the common man. (Very few, if any, women bowled before the twentieth century.) Martin Luther was an avid bowler and established the ninepin game that became standard in Germany. The game of bowling spread from Germany into Belgium, Holland, and Austria in the fifteenth, sixteenth, and seventeenth centuries. Skittles, as bowling was called in England, was introduced there in the fourteenth century. Lawn bowling, a present-day favorite of the British, had its beginning with the development of skittles.

The Dutch are credited with bringing bowling to the United States. It is not known just when this happened, but the year 1820 is accepted by most bowling historians. By 1835 bowling at pins had gained considerable popularity in the area of New York, New England, and as far south as Washington, D.C. Unfortunately, gamblers also began to take a keen interest in bowling, and in a few years they just about took over the sport. Conditions became so bad that in 1841 the Connecticut state legislature passed an act prohibiting "bowling at 9 pins," which was the standard game then. The legislative action, however, did not preclude the formation of the game of tenpins. A group of men who wanted to continue the sport without the gambling developed this new game and met to establish rules for its conduct. This meeting, which took place in 1895, marked the organization of the American Bowling Congress (ABC) and so established the group that was to shape the game as we know it today. In 1901 the ABC conducted its first national championship tournament in Chicago. These tournaments have continued through the years since then and have gained a large following. By 1942 ABC members numbered more than a million, and by 1961 membership exceeded the 4 million mark. The number of ABC members peaked at over 4.7 million in 1979. In 1990 ABC membership dropped to just over 3 million. The membership of the Women's International Bowling Congress (WIBC), which was founded in 1916 in St. Louis, Missouri, also passed the 4 million mark in 1978. Its 1990 membership was just under 3 million.

Among professional bowlers, the prizes have shown a similar increase over the years. On January 2, 1961, the biggest single bowling prize up to that time was won by Therman Gibson of Detroit; he won $78,000 on the Jackpot Bowling television show, and he picked up this huge amount by rolling six straight strikes. Del Ballard, Jr., topped Gibson's single bowling prize, earning bowling's first $100,000 check when he won the U.S. Open in Tacoma, Washington, in 1987.

Dick Weber of St. Louis occupied a unique place in bowling history for the period from 1959 to 1965. During that time he averaged $36,000 per year in tournament winnings, with a total for the period of more than $225,000. The amount was more than double that of his nearest competitor. But, then contrast that with the earnings of Mike Aulby who won $298,237 in 1989 and set a new record.

Marshall Holman leads the field for pro career earnings with $1,496,200. Other pro bowlers who have exceeded one million dollars in lifetime earnings are Mark Roth, Earl Anthony, Pete Weber, and Mike Aulby.

These earnings were gained through competing in Professional Bowlers Association (PBA) events. The PBA tours started in 1959.

The Professional Women Bowlers Association (PWBA) was the first professional women's bowling organization. Formed in 1959, the organization held its first tournament in 1960. By 1970 ten tournaments were held per year. The PWBA no longer exists.

The Ladies Pro Bowlers Tour (LPBT) originated in 1981 and secured cable television coverage in 1986. The top money earners for 1990 were Tish Johnson, who won $94,170, Leanne Barrette, who won $89,240, and Lisa Wagner, who won $58,055. Lisa Wagner leads the top career earners with a total of $436,969. She is followed by Aleta Sill with earnings of $403,361 and Lorrie Nichols with a total of $367,341.

In noting the growth of the sport in terms of the number of ABC and WIBC members, it must be remembered that the memberships of these groups represent only a fraction of the total number who bowl. The most remarkable growth in the sport has taken place since 1954. Computerized scorekeeping is the newest trend in bowling. Automatic pinsetters as well as lavish bowling establishments complete with free baby-sitting service, free lunches, and free lessons have made the sport attractive to the entire family. In their highly successful efforts to eradicate the working-class image of the past, bowling promoters now refer to the bowling surface as *lanes* rather than alleys. In 1954 there were 17 million bowlers in the United States. This number peaked at 72 million in the early eighties, and fluctuated to approximately 65 million in 1985.

By 1989 the number of bowlers had risen back to 71 million. One out of three men, women, and children in this country enjoy this great participant sport. Nine out of every ten Americans have bowled at least once in their lifetime.

Three million adult men, three million adult women, and one million youths participate annually in sanctioned leagues throughout the country.

SOME IMPORTANT DATES IN THE HISTORY OF BOWLING

5200 B.C. Egyptians engaged in a game similar to modern tenpins.

50 B.C. Bowling introduced into Europe.

300 A.D. Bowling or *kegeling* became a part of the religious activities in Germany.

1300 Skittles, a forerunner of lawn bowling, was introduced in England.

1820 Bowling introduced in the United States by the Dutch.

1841 Connecticut state legislature passed an act prohibiting "bowling at 9 pins."

1901 First national tournament conducted by the American Bowling Congress.

1916	The Women's International Bowling Congress formed.
1932	Bowling Proprietors Association of America established.
1952	ABC first approved use of automatic pinsetters.
1954	Total number of bowlers in United States estimated at 17 million.
1962	ABC approved an all-synthetic bowling pin, the first non-wood pin found acceptable.
1966	ABC and WIBC established collegiate divisions.
1975	Intercollegiate Bowling Championships (IBC) held for the first time.
1978	ABC approved the twenty-five-hundredth 300 game.
1982	Young American Bowling Alliance (YABA) organized to provide governing rules and instruction for boys and girls.
1989	Total number of bowlers in the United States estimated at 71 million.

RECORDS AND FACTS

Sources: 1991 WIBC Media Guidebook
1991 ABC Yearbook and Media Guide

Highest first game by beginner: 253, Rollie (Bud) Terrell, Bloomfield, Iowa, August 28, 1974.

Highest game without strike, spare, split, or foul: 90, Mike Doughtery, Wooster, Ohio, October 29, 1968.

Most consecutive gutter balls: 19, Richard Caplette, Danielson, Conn., September 7, 1971.

Most consecutive splits, men: 12, Dr. Glyndon Rowe, Detroit, Mich., February, 1964; women: 14, Shirley Tophigh, Las Vegas, Nev., 1968–69.

Oldest league bowler, men: 102, John Venturello, Sunrise, Fla., active, 1990; women: 102, Mollie Marier, Kansas City, Mo., through 1986–87.

Most consecutive strikes, men: 33, John Pezzin, Toledo, Ohio, March 4, 1976; women: 40, Jeanne Maiden, Solon, Ohio, 1986–87.

Most consecutive 300 games, men: 2, Al Spotts, West Reading, Pa., March 14, 1982 and February 1, 1985; women: 2, Carol Norman, Ardmore, Okla., April 7, 1986.

Most 300 games in one season, men: 12, Michael Whalin, Dayton, Ohio, 1987–88; women: 6, Leanne Barrette, Oklahoma City, Okla., 1988–90.

Youngest to roll 300 game, men: 11, John Jaszkoski, Milwaukee, Wis., March 13, 1982 American Junior Bowling Congress (AJBC); women: 16, Mary Lou Ocheskey, Kansas City, Mo., May 11, 1962 (WIBC).

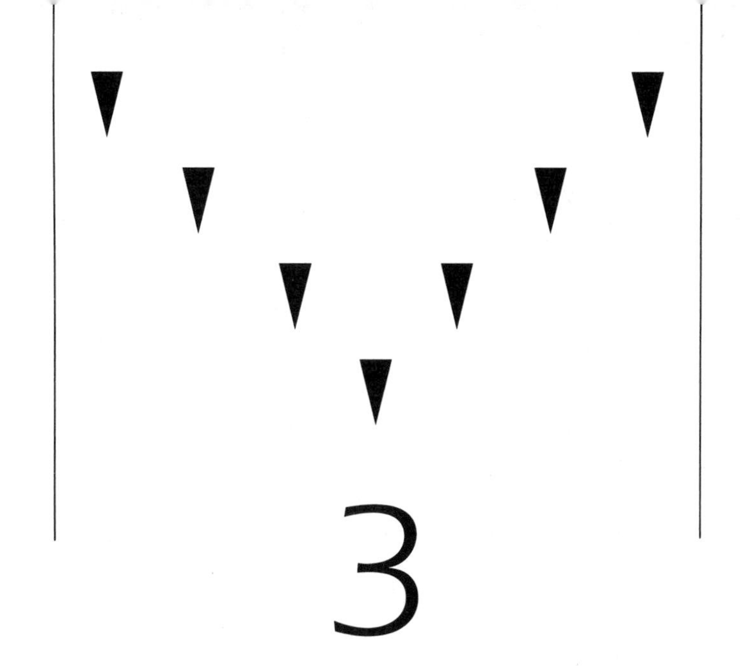

3

The Etiquette of Bowling

To completely enjoy bowling, you will feel more confident with some know-how of the generally accepted proper conduct. These rules are based on common courtesy and can be mastered easily with just a little thought. The fundamental idea is to treat others with courtesy and consideration, as you would like to be treated. This makes the game more enjoyable for everyone playing. The following are some of the more important guides to good bowling manners:

1. Check the number of the ball you have selected and use your own ball each time. It inconveniences another bowler to have to wait because you are using his or her ball.
2. Generally, you should let the bowler to your right bowl first if you are both ready at the same time. (An exception occurs when you are bowling your second ball and the bowler on the right is rolling his or her first in that frame.) When it is not your turn, stay off the approach. Also, step back and off the approach after making each delivery.

3. Be ready to bowl when it is your turn. Slowing the play, especially when you're bowling on a team, can be annoying to everyone.
4. A little needling may be part of the fun of bowling, but avoid doing it after the other person has addressed the pins; that is, taken his or her position on the lane, ready to bowl.
5. Keep refreshments away from the bench and the bowling area. A spot of soft drink on the bottom of a bowling shoe can cause a nasty fall.
6. Out of consideration for other bowlers, smoking should be avoided at the bench or in the bowling area.
7. Put your bowling shoes on before you select your bowling ball. Dirt from your street shoes should not be carried onto the lanes.
8. Control your temper. All of us experience disappointment at a missed strike or spare, but kicking the ball rack or using profanity is strictly taboo.
9. Do not loft the ball. Throwing the ball upwards so that it bounces on the lane upon delivery is not good bowling technique, and it damages the lanes.
10. When you win, enjoy it, but when you lose, don't detract from the other person's success.
11. Observe the foul line. When you foul, you lose any pins you have knocked down.
12. Limit your body movements to your own lane. Don't let your body twist after you release the ball so an arm or leg extends into an adjacent lane. It is poor follow-through technique and can be very distracting to another bowler.

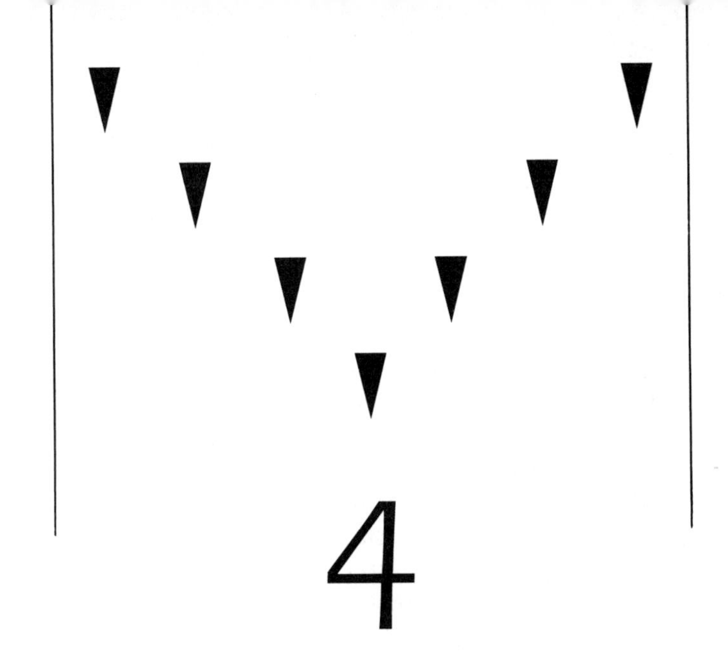

4

Bowling Terms

Like other sports, bowling has terms and phrases that are unique to that particular activity. Being familiar with these terms adds to your enjoyment and helps you become a part of the bowling scene.

Address Position Establishing your starting position on the lane prior to taking your first step.
Anchor Person The last person in the line-up of a team.
Approach The area across which the bowler steps prior to delivering the ball at the foul line.
Arrows Triangular-shaped aiming points. Also called *spots.*
Auditory Cues Key words or catch phrases that present a concept.
Baby Split The 2–7 or 3–10 split.
Backup A ball that curves left to right for a right-hander, right to left for a left-hander.
Bedposts The 7–10 split.
Blind Score given a team for an absent member.
Blow Failing to make a spare except in the case of a split that cannot normally be made. Also called an *error* or *miss.*

Board One of the one-inch boards making up each lane.
Brooklyn Hit A ball that rolls into the pocket on the wrong side of the head pin. Also called a *crossover* or *Jersey* hit.
Channel A more modern term for the *gutter.*
Cherry *See* **Chop.**
Chop Knocking down the front pin on a spare attempt, leaving adjacent pins standing. Also called a *cherry.*
Convert When you successfully make your spare.
Count The number of pins knocked down with the first ball.
Creeper A very slow ball.
Crossover *See* **Brooklyn Hit.**
Cues *See* **Auditory Cues** and **Visual Cues.**
Curve A ball that has a wide and sweeping arc, more pronounced than a hook.
Dead Ball A poorly rolled ball that has little action—that doesn't take down as many pins as a "live" ball.
Double Two strikes in a row.
Error A blow or miss.
Fast Lane A lane on which the hook ball does not curve or "take" as much as usual.
Foul Touching or going beyond the foul line when the bowler delivers the ball.
Foul Line The line that separates the approach from the lane.
Four Bagger Four strikes in a row.
Frame The box on the scoresheet in which the score is recorded; also one-tenth of a game.
Gutter Channels on both sides of each lane.
Gutterball A ball that goes off the lane into the gutter.
Handicap A scoring advantage that lets individuals or teams of different averages compete in the same league.
Head Pin The 1 pin, which is the pin closest to the bowler.
High Hit A strike ball that hits more of the 1 pin or head pin than the 1–3 pocket.
Hook A ball that breaks to the left for a right-hander or to the right for a left-hander.
Kegler A synonym for *bowler,* derived from the German word *kegel.*

Kingpin The 5 pin.
Lane A synonym for *alley.*
Leadoff Person The first bowler in a team line-up.
Leave The pins that remain standing after the first ball is rolled in a frame.
Line A game of ten frames.
Live Ball A ball that knocks down a lot of pins even though it may miss the pocket.
Lofting Throwing the ball too far out on the lane so that it bounces.
Mark A strike or spare.
Open Frame A frame without a strike or a spare.
Perfect Game A score of 300 resulting from 12 consecutive strikes.
Pin Action The manner in which the pins fall, depending on the speed and spin of the ball.
Pin Bowling Using the pins as aiming points.
Pocket The area defined by the 1–3 pins for right-handers; the 1–2 for left-handers.
Pushaway The extension of your arms as you push the ball out from your body when taking your first step.
Railroad *See* **Split.**
Scratch Bowler A bowler who has no handicap.
Sleeper A pin hidden behind another pin.
Span Distance between thumbhole and finger holes.
Spare Knocking down all ten pins with two balls in a frame.
Split A leave in which the head pin is down and two or more pins remain standing with adjacent pins knocked down in front and between; also known as a *railroad.*
Spots Dark-colored, triangular-shaped arrowheads on the bowling lane itself.
Spot Bowling Using the arrowheads or spots as aiming points.
Strike Knocking down all pins with the first ball.
Strike Out To get three strikes in the tenth and final frame.
Sweeper A live ball that sweeps the pins off the lane.
Tap Leaving a 10, 4, or 7 pin on what appeared to be a strike ball.
Thin Hit A hit in which the ball barely contacts the 1 pin. Also called a *light hit.*

Turkey Three strikes in a row.

Visual Cues Images of proper approach techniques that you picture yourself doing.

Washout The 1–2–4–10 leave for a right-hander; the 1–3–6–7 leave for a left-hander.

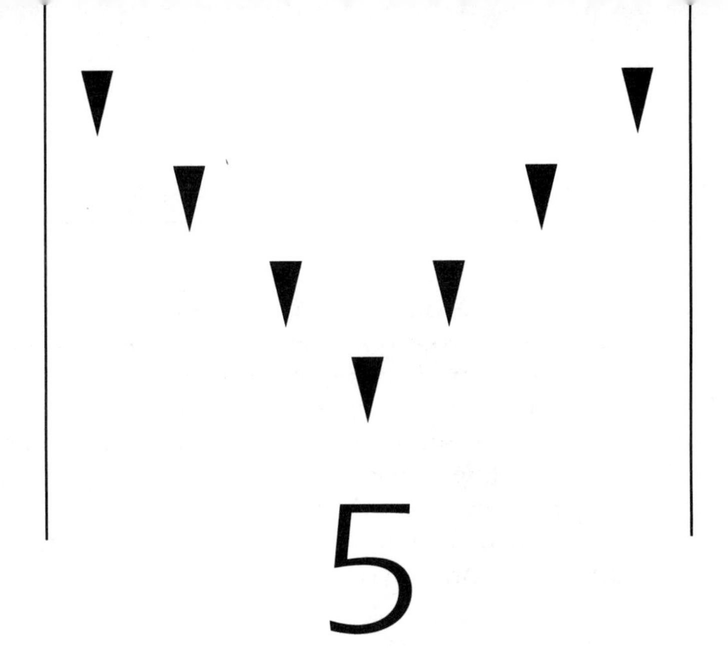

5

Tips for Beginners

When you visit a bowling establishment, you'll notice almost as many different styles and techniques as there are bowlers. Even among experts, individual refinements will vary a lot, although there will be some basic similarities. Certain questions may occur to you: How do I select a ball? Should I use a three-, four-, or five-step delivery? Is a hook better than a straight ball? When you listen to the conversation of bowlers, you may become even more confused by hearing such terms as *spot bowling, pin bowling, backup ball,* and *curve*. The following section is designed to eliminate some of this confusion and to provide you with some guidelines for a good start at learning the skills of bowling.

WARMUP ACTIVITY

Bowling may not appear to be a very physical sport. But, it's easy to strain muscles when you carry and roll a ball weighing from 8 to 16 pounds without first having warmed up. The first step in warming up is to do some vigorous walking. This can be done on the way to the bowling establishment or after you arrive. The second step is to swing your arms in circles out to the side of your body, then in front of your body. Finally, swing arms in back of your body. Start slowly with small circles then, increase the speed and size of your circles. Continue your exercises until your body begins to feel warm. Next, with your bowling hand, make a fist and then extend your fingers. Repeat this several times.

Your warmup activity will lessen the chance of muscle strain or injury and improve your skill performance.

SELECTING YOUR BALL

The weight of a bowling ball varies from 8 to 16 pounds, as determined by the rules of the American Bowling Congress. Most men use the 16-pound ball, although a lighter ball is recommended if you have difficulty with control. Women generally improve their accuracy using a lighter ball, although many women can also handle a 15- or 16-pound ball. Again, control is the key point to keep in mind. Here is the specific technique by which to select your ball (see Figure 5-1).

First, make sure your thumb will slip in and out of the thumbhole easily. Second, with your thumb in the thumbhole, lay your hand across the ball but do not put your fingers into the finger holes. The knuckles of your middle two fingers should be directly over the inside edge of the finger holes. When you insert the thumb and the two middle fingers into the holes, there should be just enough space between your palm and the ball for a pencil to fit snugly. This is the simplest way to determine the correct span. If you purchase your own ball, your bowling proprietor will take more exact measurements. There's no doubt that having your own properly fitted ball is a definite asset in developing consistency.

HANDLING YOUR BALL

Here's a tip to avoid getting a smashed finger. When you pick up your ball from the rack, face the pins and place *both* hands on either side of the ball so if another ball hits yours,

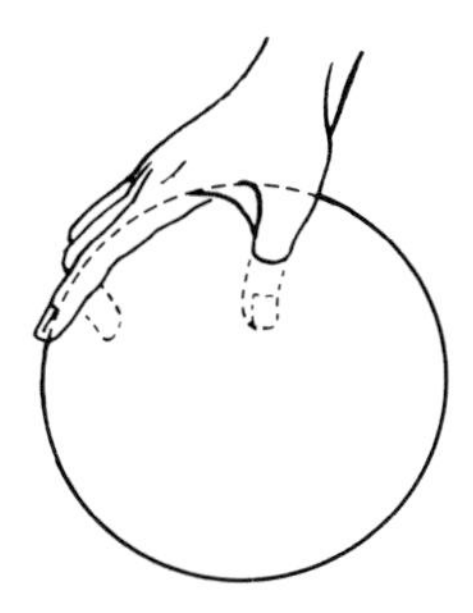

1. Your thumb should slip in and out of the thumbhole rather easily.

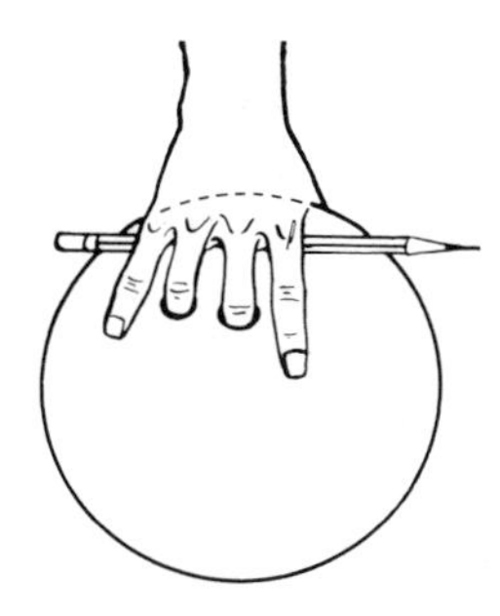

3. There ought to be just enough space under your palm for a pencil to fit snugly.

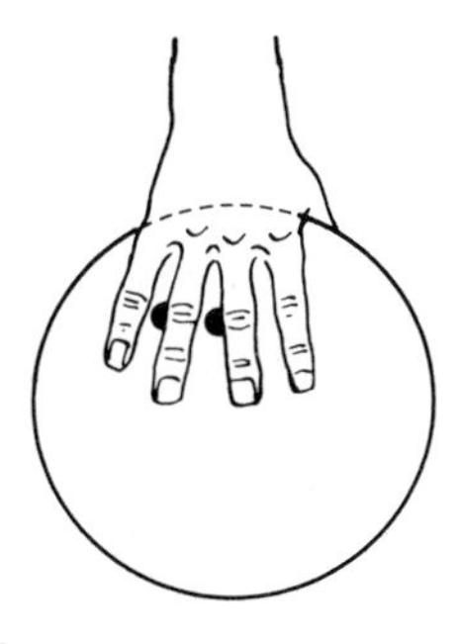

2. For proper span, the knuckles of your middle fingers should be over the edges of the finger holes with your thumb in the thumbhole.

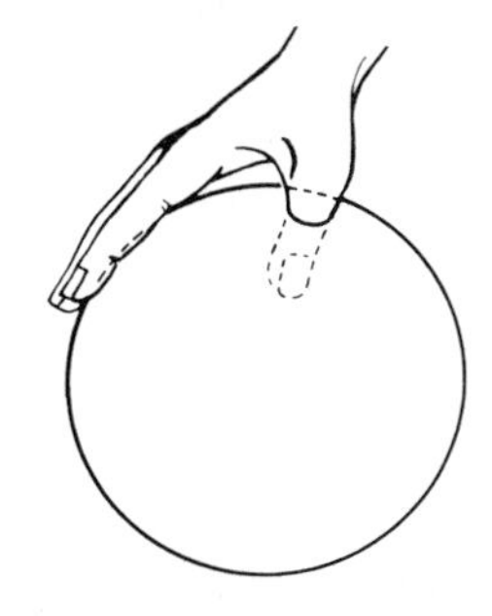

4. Only by actually using the ball can you determine whether the fit is correct.

FIGURE 5-1
SELECTING YOUR BALL

your fingers won't be in the way. Then, lift the ball with both hands. Don't pick up the ball by putting your fingers in the finger holes. If you do, you'll lift up to 300 pounds in one game with just three fingers. Hand fatigue and loss of control are the direct results.

THREE-, FOUR-, OR FIVE-STEP DELIVERY

All three types of delivery are being used with effectiveness; however, the four-step delivery (see Chapter 6) is suggested for beginners, as well as for more advanced bowlers. It is smoother, provides better balance than the three-step variety, and is less complicated than the five-step delivery.

THE STRAIGHT BALL VERSUS THE HOOK BALL, THE CURVE, OR THE BACKUP

The straight ball is delivered from a position toward the right side of the approach directly into the 1–3 pocket (see Figure 5-2). It has no sideward spin and so does not curve to the left or right. It is probably the most easily controlled of the group, but most bowling authorities recommend the hook ball, even for beginners. The spot bowling system presented in Chapter 8 applies to both straight and hook balls.

The hook ball and the curve ball, when delivered properly, provide better action (knock down more pins) than the straight ball. To roll a hook, the ball is released with the hand in a handshake position. This puts a counterclockwise spin on the ball, causing it to curve left. (For left-handers, of course, the directions are reversed.) Your instructor will help you decide if you are ready to learn the hook delivery. It may be that you will show a natural hook right from the start of instruction, or your instructor may prefer that you start out with the hook rather than a straight ball. More detailed information about the hook ball is included in Chapter 13, "Advanced Techniques: The Hook Ball."

The backup ball is the result of either faulty delivery or a natural tendency to throw a ball that curves from left to right. Some people have a natural backup ball. Faults that cause this include turning the hand in a clockwise manner as the ball is released or pulling the hand up and to the right in the follow-through. Your instructor can help you decide whether your

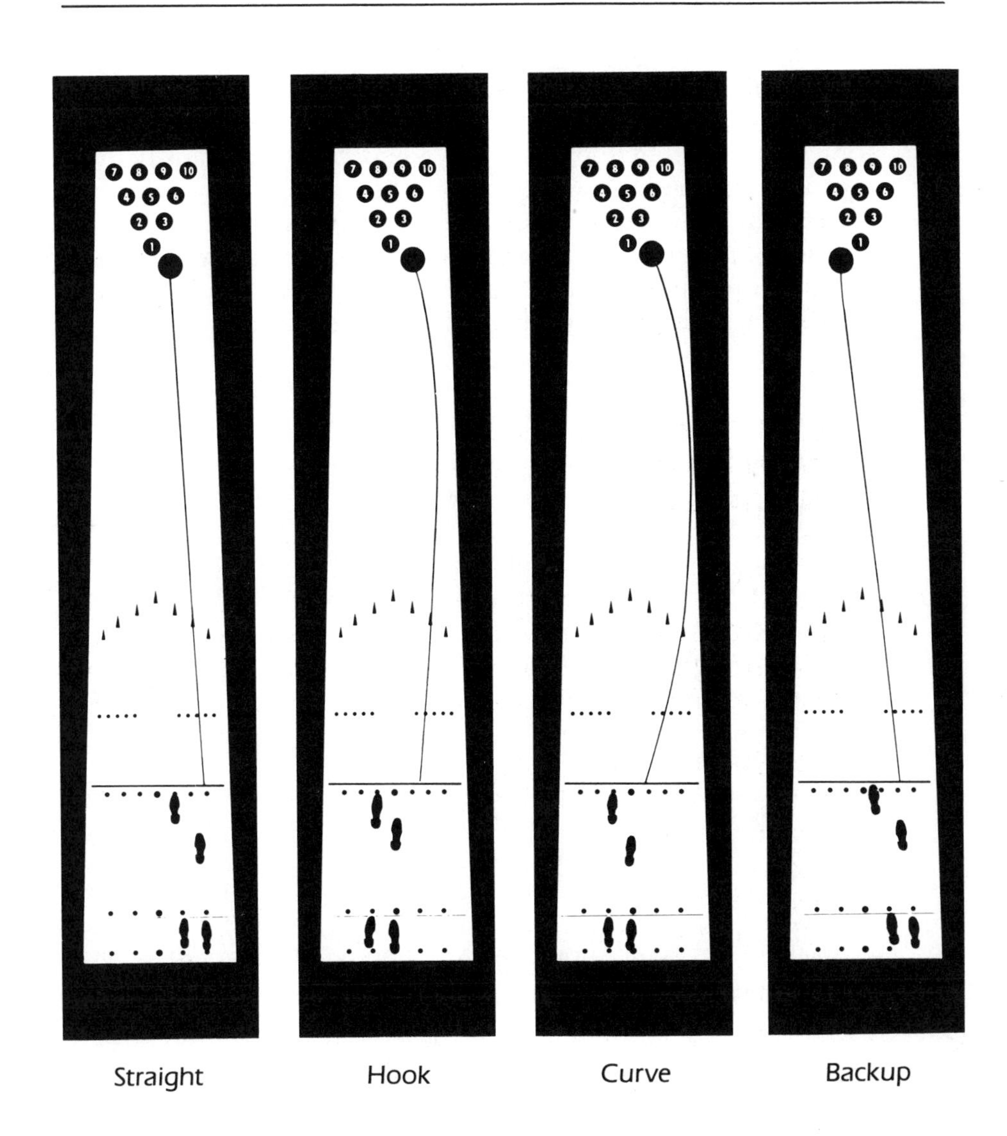

FIGURE 5-2
TYPES OF DELIVERY

Note: Drawings not to scale.

backup ball is natural and reasonably effective or whether it needs correcting. It is true that the left-to-right curve can produce good action, but only when consistency of delivery can be attained.

Figure 5-3 illustrates the hand positions at the moment of release for the straight, hook, curve, and backup balls. Note that the position of the thumb for the straight ball is at twelve o'clock, while the ring finger of the right hand points to six o'clock. The hand is rotated to the left for the hook, with the thumb at ten o'clock and the ring finger at four o'clock. Thus, to progress from a straight ball to a slight hook, the thumb is positioned at eleven o'clock and the ring finger at five o'clock. Additional rotation to the left creates the curve hand position. The thumb is at nine o'clock and the ring finger at three o'clock. Finally, the backup hand position finds the thumb at one o'clock and the third finger at seven o'clock.

FAST LANES

A fast lane is one on which your hook ball does not curve or take as much as usual. The lessened curve is caused by a lack of friction that reduces the sideward spin of the ball. A highly polished, glassy surface may be your tip-off to a fast lane, but you won't really know until you have thrown a few balls. If your ball misses the 1–3 pocket to the right on each practice roll, you should move slightly to the right of your usual starting position. As Chapter 8 on spot bowling explains, this will shift the path of your ball slightly to the left.

SLOW LANES

If, on your practice rolls, your ball curves to the left of the 1–3 pocket and hits pins to the left of the head pin, you may be on a slow lane. Increased friction on the lane causes an exaggeration of your hook ball. Dust on your ball or on the lanes could also cause a slow-lane condition. Move slightly to the left of your normal starting position to make the necessary adjustment.

Straight

Thumb at twelve o'clock;
ring finger at six o'clock.

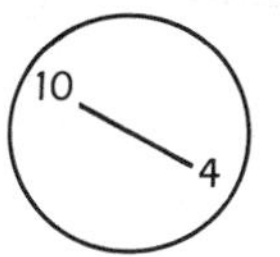

Hook

Thumb at ten o'clock;
ring finger at four o'clock.

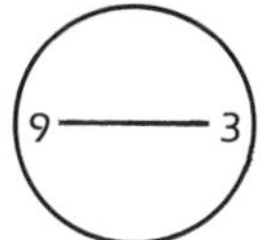

Curve

Thumb at nine o'clock;
ring finger at three o'clock.

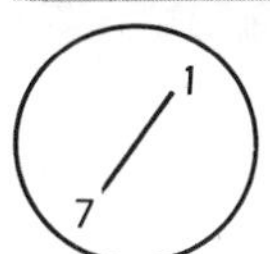

Backup

Thumb at one o'clock;
ring finger at seven o'clock.

FIGURE 5-3
HAND POSITIONS FOR DIFFERENT DELIVERIES

SPEED AND BALL WEIGHT AS THEY AFFECT PIN ACTION

The two factors relating to the action that results when your ball hits the pins are the speed and weight of your ball. High-speed photography has shown that the extremely fast ball lifts the pins vertically and therefore reduces pin action. The ball delivered with moderate speed causes the front pins to fall sideways, and these in turn cause other pins to fall. Additional pin action results from the spinning.

Another factor related to the speed of the ball is the mechanics of ball action. A study done by the American Bowling Congress reveals the following data: When a ball leaves your hand, it does three things as it travels down the lane. It skids—slides forward without spinning or rotating; rolls—rotates forward in the direction of the pins; and takes—spins in such a way to cause the ball to hook, back up, or continue in a straight line (see Table 5-1). A normal ball has 20 feet of take, a slow ball 30 feet of take. That is why a slow ball fades and dies, causing 8–10, 5-pin, and other leaves. The ball dies or loses its spin before it reaches the pins.

The fast ball has a skid of 30 feet. Its roll is the same as the others at 25 feet, but it has only 5 feet of take. If you throw a hook ball and throw with too much speed, your ball will lose some of its sideward spin and therefore some of its action.

Here are ways to change the speed of your ball.

To increase speed

1. Hold the ball higher in address position.
2. Increase the length of your pushaway (the extension of your arms as you push the ball out from your body when taking your first step).
3. Speed up your approach.
4. Lengthen your approach.

To decrease speed

1. Hold ball lower in address position.
2. Shorten your pushaway.
3. Slow your approach.
4. Shorten your approach.

TABLE 5-1
MECHANICS OF BALL ACTION

	Normal speed (feet)	Too fast (feet)	Too slow (feet)
Skids	15	30	5
Rolls	25	25	25
Takes	20	5	30
Total	60	60	60

The weight of your ball is related to pin action. If your ball is too light, it will be deflected so much that pin action will be reduced. This is especially true if your ball also lacks sufficient velocity. Women sometimes have the problem of using a light ball and then lacking the strength to develop adequate speed. The combination of these two factors may cause a good pocket hit to take down only seven or eight pins. Using a slightly heavier ball or increasing the ball velocity by means of the suggestions above will correct this problem.

A good principle for both men and women is to use the heaviest ball you can control and yet still develop moderate speed. Swing the ball back and forth in a trial swing without dropping your shoulder, to tell if you can handle the ball without losing control.

SPOT VERSUS PIN BOWLING

There are advocates of both spot and pin methods of bowling, but most topflight bowlers use the spot-bowling technique. The essential difference is really quite simple: In pin bowling, your point of aim is the pins themselves; in spot bowling, the point of aim, the *spot,* is either a dot or triangular-shaped "arrowhead" located a short distance from the foul line. There is a more detailed discussion of spot bowling in Chapter 8.

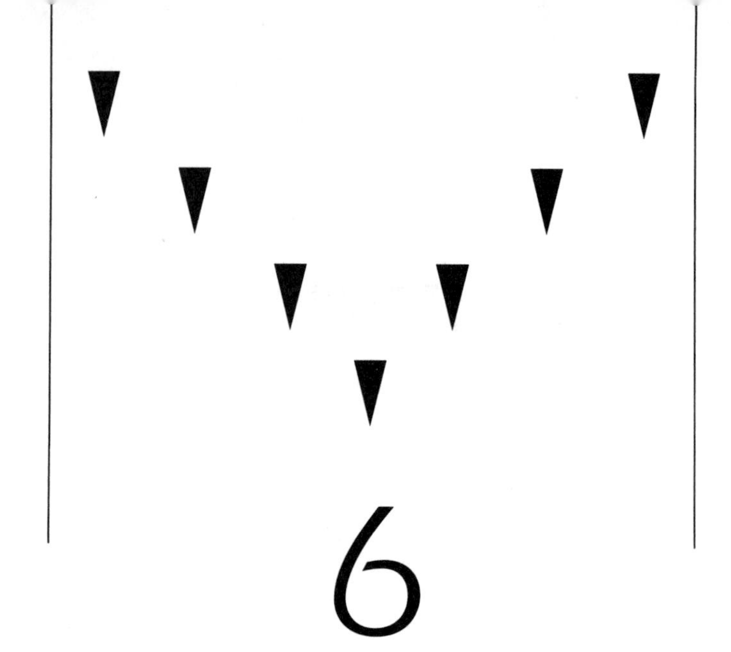

6

Learning Bowling Through Audio-Visual Cues

What is the best way to learn how to roll a bowling ball properly? How do you do the pushaway, follow through correctly, hit the pocket, develop good form, and obtain consistent results? And finally, how can you accomplish all the other essentials of good bowling technique?

The answer is *cues*—auditory and visual cues. Auditory cues are key words or catch phrases that present a concept. These cues include written words as well as the descriptions given by your instructor. With respect to the approach, for example, the phrase "perfect balance is essential to good bowling" is an auditory cue.

Visual cues, on the other hand, use checkpoints for ease in learning and remembering key movements or positions. A checkpoint or visual cue on the proper approach technique is the image of the ball being pushed away with your right arm fully extended as you take your first step. Visual cues refer to things that you can see for yourself.

These are just two illustrations of how audio-visual cues can be used. What follows is a discussion of how these techniques can help you learn the fundamental skills of the game. (Note that some cues must be reversed to apply to left-handers.) I have included several basic aspects of bowling: starting position, approach, and release of the ball. Let's look at them.

STARTING POSITION

Auditory Cues

1. Hold your body erect.
2. Shift your weight to your left foot.
3. Maintain a relaxed position.
4. To find your starting position, walk four and one-half steps back from the foul line.
5. Flex your knees slightly and shift your weight onto the balls of your feet.

Visual Cues or Checkpoints

1. Keep your feet far enough apart to maintain good balance and point your toes straight ahead.
2. Keep your right foot back of the left foot so that your right toe is opposite the midpoint of your left foot.
3. Hold the ball in a waist-high position in line with your right hip. (See Figure 6-1.)
4. The palm of your right hand should face your chest with your thumb in the twelve-o'clock position to roll a straight ball. If you roll a hook, your palm should face to the left with your thumb in the ten-o'clock position. (See Figures 6-2 and 6-3.)
5. Place your left hand beneath the ball on the left side for support. Your little fingers should be touching each other.

Hold the ball in a waist-high position in line with right hip.

FIGURE 6-1

To roll a straight ball, hold your palm toward your chest with your thumb in the twelve-o'clock position.

FIGURE 6-2

To roll a hook, hold your palm toward the left with your thumb in the ten-o'clock position.

FIGURE 6-3

6. With your right hand and wrist, form a straight line with your forearm.
7. Keep your right elbow snug against your body.

APPROACH

Auditory Cues

1. Perfect balance is essential to good bowling.
2. Walk straight toward the target.
3. Don't rush your delivery.
4. Try to develop a smooth approach and release.
5. Use shuffle steps as in ballroom dancing.
6. A medium-fast ball is more effective than one "thrown through the back of the building."

Visual Cues or Checkpoints

1. Your first step should be a short one taken with your right foot (see Figure 6-4).
2. As you take your first step, the ball should be pushed away and both arms fully extended (see Figure 6-4).
3. Your left arm should assist your right in the pushaway.
4. As you complete the pushaway, drop your left hand off the ball and move your arm to the side to counterbalance the weight of the ball. Allow the ball to swing downward in a pendulum motion (see Figures 6-5 and 6-6).
5. The pendulum swing should continue until the ball has swung back past your body to a waist-high position (see Figure 6-7).
6. The remainder of the steps—four in all—should be done without specific concern for the position of the ball. The pendulum movement should be done without tightness or tension (see Figures 6-8 and 6-9).

Your first step should be a short one taken with your right foot. As you step, push the ball away and fully extend both arms.

FIGURE 6-4

As you complete the pushaway, drop your left hand off the ball. Allow your ball to swing down in a pendulum motion while you take the second step.

FIGURE 6-5

Continue your pendulum motion as you start to take the third step.

FIGURE 6-6

Let the ball swing past your body to a waist-high position.

FIGURE 6-7

7. Your final step with your left foot, a sliding motion forward, should take place as you complete the forward swing of the ball (see Figure 6-10).
8. Keep a firm wrist throughout the swing.

RELEASE OF THE BALL

Auditory Cues

1. Deliver the ball with smoothness and accuracy.
2. Correct follow-through is a key to consistent good bowling.
3. Good balance, important throughout the approach, is the essence of an accurate delivery.

Visual Cues or Checkpoints

1. On your final or fourth step, place your left foot next to your right and slide it straight forward.
2. Flex your left knee at a 90-degree angle as you complete the slide forward.
3. Point both feet straight down the alley.
4. Keep your body erect from the waist up.
5. Keep your shoulders square to the foul line.
6. Release the ball at a point in front of your left foot and in line with your right shoulder.
7. At the moment of release, keep your wrist straight and your thumb in the correct position (see Figure 6-10).
8. In the follow-through, point your hand straight down the alley.
9. As you release the ball, pull your hand up to ear height to obtain more spin on your ball (see Figure 6-11).
10. To ensure proper balance, maintain the follow-through position for several seconds.
11. Watch your ball to see if it rolls over the proper spot or arrowhead.

The final part of the four-step delivery should be done without specific concern for the position of the ball.

FIGURE 6-8

Swing the ball forward without tightness or tension.

FIGURE 6-9

Your final step is a slide. At the moment of release, keep your wrist straight and your thumb in position.

FIGURE 6-10

As you release the ball, pull your hand up to ear height to obtain more spin on your ball.

FIGURE 6-11

MENTAL PRACTICE

Mental practice involving mental imagery has become an important addition to the skill development for athletes in a variety of sports. The first step in developing mental practice skills is learning a relaxation technique, such as the one that follows:

1. Find a quiet place to relax, away from noise and other people.
2. Get in comfortable position. Sit in a comfortable chair. Lying down could work also, but if you fall asleep, a vivid dream could distract you from relaxing.
3. Focus on your breathing. Repeat the words *inhale* and *exhale* to yourself as you breathe. Put your hand on your abdomen as you inhale. Feel your abdomen rise, then your chest, and then your shoulders as you slowly take a deep breath. Then, as you exhale feel your shoulders go down, your chest go down, and your abdomen go in. As you do this concentrate on the words *inhale* and *exhale*. You will find that you will gradually block out all other thoughts and zero in on the words *inhale* and *exhale*.

The first time you practice this relaxation technique do it for just five minutes. Gradually increase the time to ten minutes.

The benefits of learning the relaxation technique apply to more than just improving your skill in sports or, in this case, bowling. You are learning how to block out unpleasant or troublesome thoughts, thus enabling yourself to deal more effectively with life's stressful happenings.

Once you've learned the relaxation technique you can begin to apply mental imagery to improving your bowling skills. But in order to use mental imagery to improve your skill, you must have an accurate mental concept of the correct movements used to roll the bowling ball down the lane. Thus, mental imagery is not effective with the beginning bowler until they understand the basic skills. If you're a beginner, ask your bowling instructor to videotape you rolling the ball. Then have your instructor analyze the tape and point out what changes need to be made. Then you can concentrate on these as you practice mental imagery.

APPLICATION OF MENTAL IMAGERY TO BOWLING SKILLS

Here's how you apply mental imagery to bowling:

1. Go through the relaxation technique.
2. Shift your concentration from the words *inhale* and *exhale* to a visualization of your rolling a bowling ball down the lane. Focus on the auditory and visual cues presented earlier in this chapter. For example: Visualize the actions "hold your body erect; shift your weight to your left foot; flex your knees slightly and shift your weight onto the balls of your feet." Then visualize the whole sequence as you look at your spot on the lane and move forward to release the ball. Include also your feelings as you go through this sequence. Recreate the feelings you have as you release the ball, watch it go over your target spot, continue down the lane, hit the 1–3 pocket, and have a strike. Imagine the sound as the ball goes in the pocket. Practice this visualization for both strikes and spares.
3. Keep your imagery practice session short, five to ten minutes. Practice regularly. Keep in mind that relaxed concentration is a learned process that must be practiced to be a regular part of your learning experience.

In doing your visualization, it is helpful to think back to when you did roll a strike or convert a spare and to try to duplicate that experience in your mind. If you have been working on a change in your bowling skill that your instructor has pointed out to you, work this into your visual imagery.

When you are actually bowling, visualize the correct technique as you are waiting your turn. If you're having a bad day on the lane, visualize the feelings you had when you were having a good day. Repeat to yourself an auditory cue, for example, "hold the follow through and maintain perfect balance."

As you wait your turn to bowl use mental rehearsal. Prepare yourself by bringing a picture to your mind of the correct technique you are about to use. If, when you are actually bowling, you roll a ball off-target, shift your concentration to the correct technique in preparation for your next delivery.

Remember the old saying, "Practice makes perfect"? Mental practice may not make you perfect, but it certainly can help you improve your bowling skills.

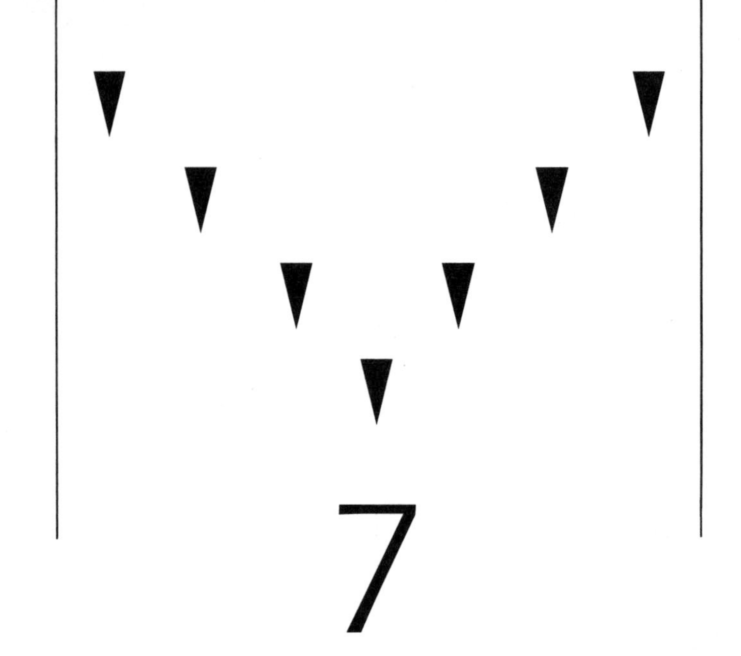

7

Common Faults and How to Correct Them

Before you can correct errors you must understand the causes. If your ball deviates from the path you intended it to take, there are three and *only* three causes. They involve your hand, your arm, and your body. First, instead of having your hand in a position at release so your thumb was at ten o'clock and your ring finger at five o'clock, you twisted your hand counterclockwise. Your thumb ended up at nine o'clock, your ball curved left too much, and you missed your target.

Or perhaps you twisted your hand clockwise and your thumb ended up at one o'clock and a backup ball resulted. Now your ball curved to the right, and you missed the pins.

Let's take a look at your arm movement. If your arm crosses your body and finishes way left of straight ahead, the ball will be off-target to the left. Likewise, if your arm finishes to the right of a position straight ahead, your ball will go to the right of your target.

Finally, your body position at the moment of release affects the roll of your ball. Your shoulders should be square to the foul line. If they are turned to the left, that's probably the direction your ball will go. If they face to the right, your ball will head that way.

So, there you have it—deviations from your target line due to errors in hand, arm, or body action. How do you correct your errors? First, you have your instructor analyze your delivery to determine which error you are making. Then with your instructor's help, use these tips for correcting the errors:

HAND ERROR

Go through the sequence without the ball. Say to yourself, "Keep a thumb at ten o'clock. Ready, pushaway, down, back, and through into high finish." Then actually walk through it. Look at your hand as you finish your follow-through. Your hand should be head-high. Ask a partner to watch you go through it without the ball and then with a ball. Hold the finish for five counts each time so your partner can check it.

ARM ERROR

Use a partner for this one, too. Do it first without the ball and then with it. As you follow through, touch your thumb to your right ear. This will ensure that your arm has followed through in a straight line toward your target. "Freeze" in the follow-through position so your partner can check your finish position.

BODY ERROR

The important thing is to keep your shoulders square to the foul line and maintain good balance. Your left arm should be extended to the side as a counterbalance. Again, your partner can be very helpful. "Freeze" in the follow-through position until your partner taps you on the shoulder. Count to yourself: "One thousand one, one thousand two, one thousand three, one thousand four, one thousand five." Take a look at your shoulders as you hold the position. Are they square to the foul line? Maintaining good balance is the key to consistency in bowling. This fact cannot be stressed too much.

All the errors and corrections described here are related to the basic mechanics of rolling a bowling ball. The greatest professional athletes in all sports concentrate most on basic mechanics.

RHYTHM AND TIMING PROBLEMS

Once you have made good progress on eliminating basic errors of hand, arm, and body, you can begin to focus on improving the action of your ball. As noted on page 22 the ball skids, rolls, and then takes after it leaves your hand. Many bowlers release the ball right at the foul line. In doing so, much of the rotation of the ball, which is necessary for good action, is gone by the time the ball reaches the pins.

The ball should be laid out on the lane about 15 to 18 inches beyond the foul line. You can check your ball contact point by placing a piece of standard white typing paper or a towel so it covers the area of 15 to 18 inches beyond the foul line. Your ball will make a mark on the paper if you don't get it far enough out on the lane. Failure to get the ball far enough out on the lane is caused by your left foot arriving at the foul line before your arm is in a position to release the ball. This is usually the result of the following errors: (1) starting your first step before you push the ball out and down or (2) pushing the ball out and then pausing for half a step before you allow it to go down in a pendular movement.

The solution to the problem is to start your pushaway just slightly before you take your first step. Push the ball out and down and let the weight of the ball carry your arm through a pendulum movement. Use the paper on the lane to check your progress. Improved pin action is the direct result of your improved timing.

Another common error is rushing to the foul line. Make your first step a short one and glide smoothly toward your target.

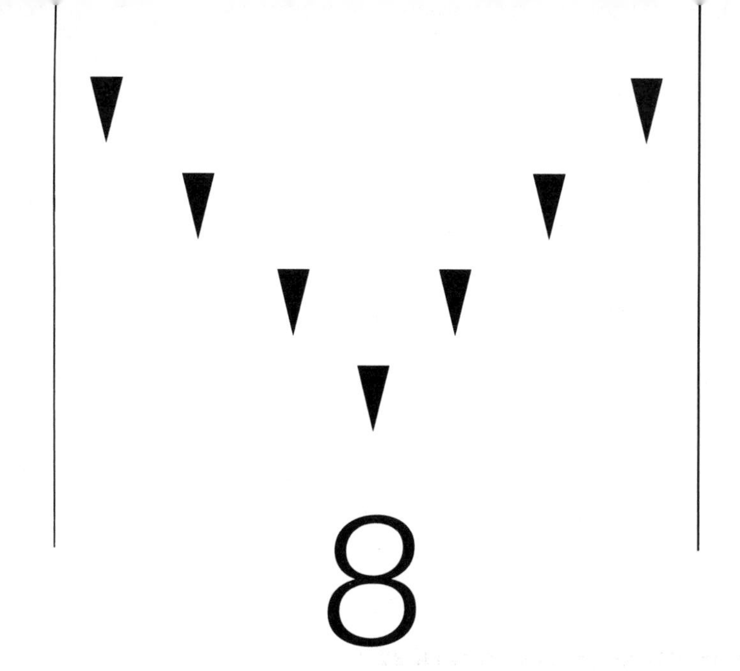

8

Improving Your Score Through Spot Bowling

Do you need to be convinced that spot bowling is better than pin bowling? If so, consider these facts: (1) nine out of ten professionals use the spot-bowling method; (2) your concentration is more effective at 15 feet than at 60 to 65 feet; (3) you have less peripheral vision with a closer target and are therefore less affected by distractions in the immediate vicinity; and (4) a pin bowler is a spot bowler who does not look at the spot—a pin bowler must, however, roll over a spot to hit the target. Convinced? You probably will be as you master the technique. Here are the principles you need to understand and master.

ROLLING FOR STRIKES

Let's start out by helping you roll a strike ball using this technique (see Figure 8-1). On the approach area you will notice three rows of dots that run parallel to the foul line. You will also notice some dark-colored, triangular-shaped pieces of wood, called spots, on the lane itself. A point between the 1 and 3 pins (or the 1–3 pocket) is our target for a strike ball. We are concerned with lining up three things: a starting position on the approach area, one of the spots on the lane, and the 1–3 pocket. We can definitely establish two of these right away. The second spot from the right will be your target on the lane and, of course, we want the ball to hit the 1–3 pocket. Now we need to determine the exact place for you to stand in order to roll the ball over the spot and into the strike zone. You can start out by assuming an approximate position and then adjusting yourself to discover the precise place. If you are a straight-ball bowler, you should start by placing your right foot on a board that is in line with the dot on the right side of the approach area (see Figures 8-1 and 8-2). Your actual distance from the foul line will vary according to the length of your steps. If you roll a hook, you will need to move left of the dot two or more boards (see Figure 8-1).

Now, you should sight down the lane and form an imaginary line from your position through the second spot and into the 1–3 pocket. When you are ready to bowl, concentrate on the second spot from the right, not on the pins. As you release the ball, try to roll it right over that second spot. If you succeed in rolling the ball over the spot and into the pocket for a good hit, the place you started from is the correct one for you. If, however, your ball did roll over the spot but missed the pocket, you will need to adjust your starting position. The last illustration of Figure 8-1 shows how the second spot acts as pivot point. Therefore, if you have missed the pocket on the right side, you move one board to your right from your original starting position. If you have missed the pocket on the left, you should move left one board. By doing this, you can determine your exact starting place. If you are having any difficulty, ask your instructor for help.

The key to spot bowling is consistency. To be successful, you must be able to roll the ball over a precise spot, and this is not easy at first. But your score and confidence will both go up once you achieve this valuable skill.

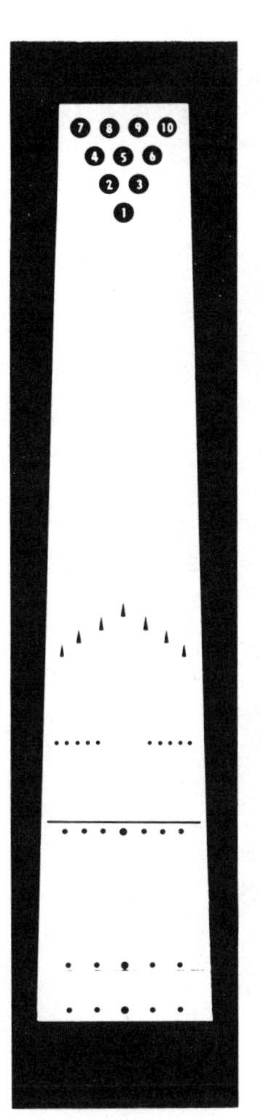

The second arrowhead from the right is the target spot.

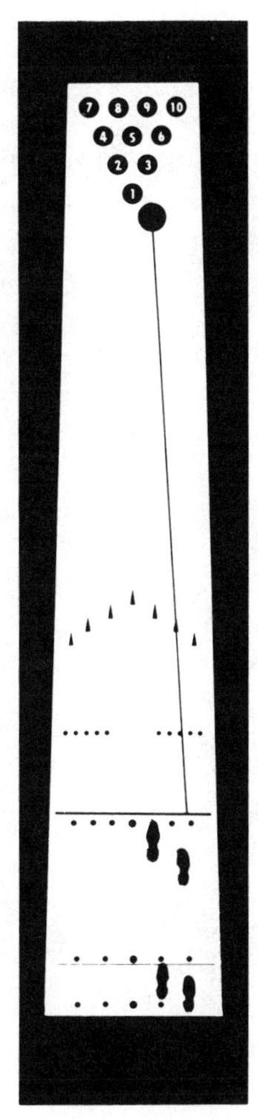

Straight-ball bowlers make a delivery from the right side.

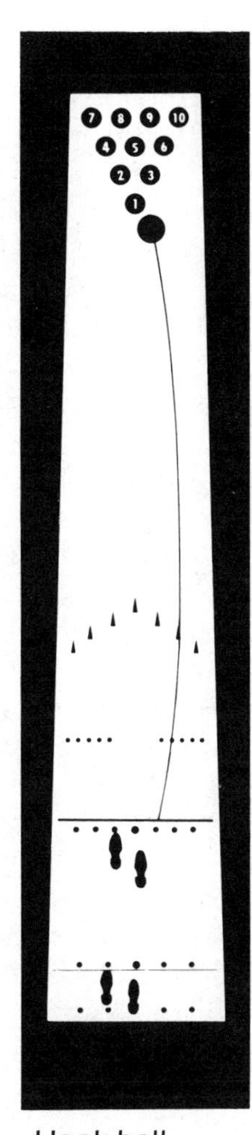

Hook-ball bowlers move the starting position to the left.

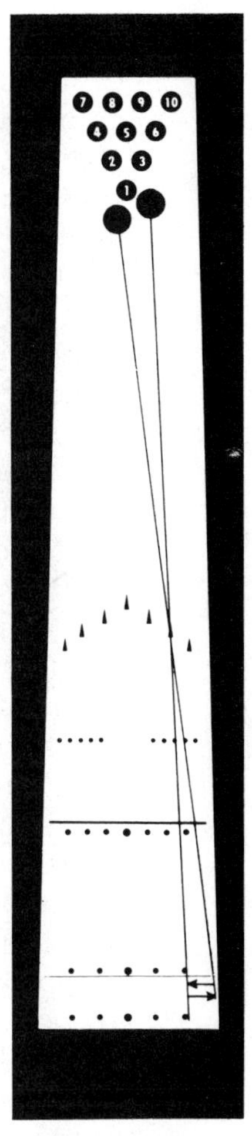

Adjust to find your exact starting position.

FIGURE 8-1

SPOT BOWLING FOR STRIKES

FIGURE 8-2
FOOT POSITION FOR STRIKE BALL

PICKING UP SPARES

Using the basic strike position, it is an easy matter to pick up certain middle spares with the straight ball. You can pick up the 5 pin, the 5–8 spare, the 1–2–5 spare, and the 1–2–9 spare merely by rolling the strike ball (see Figure 8-3).

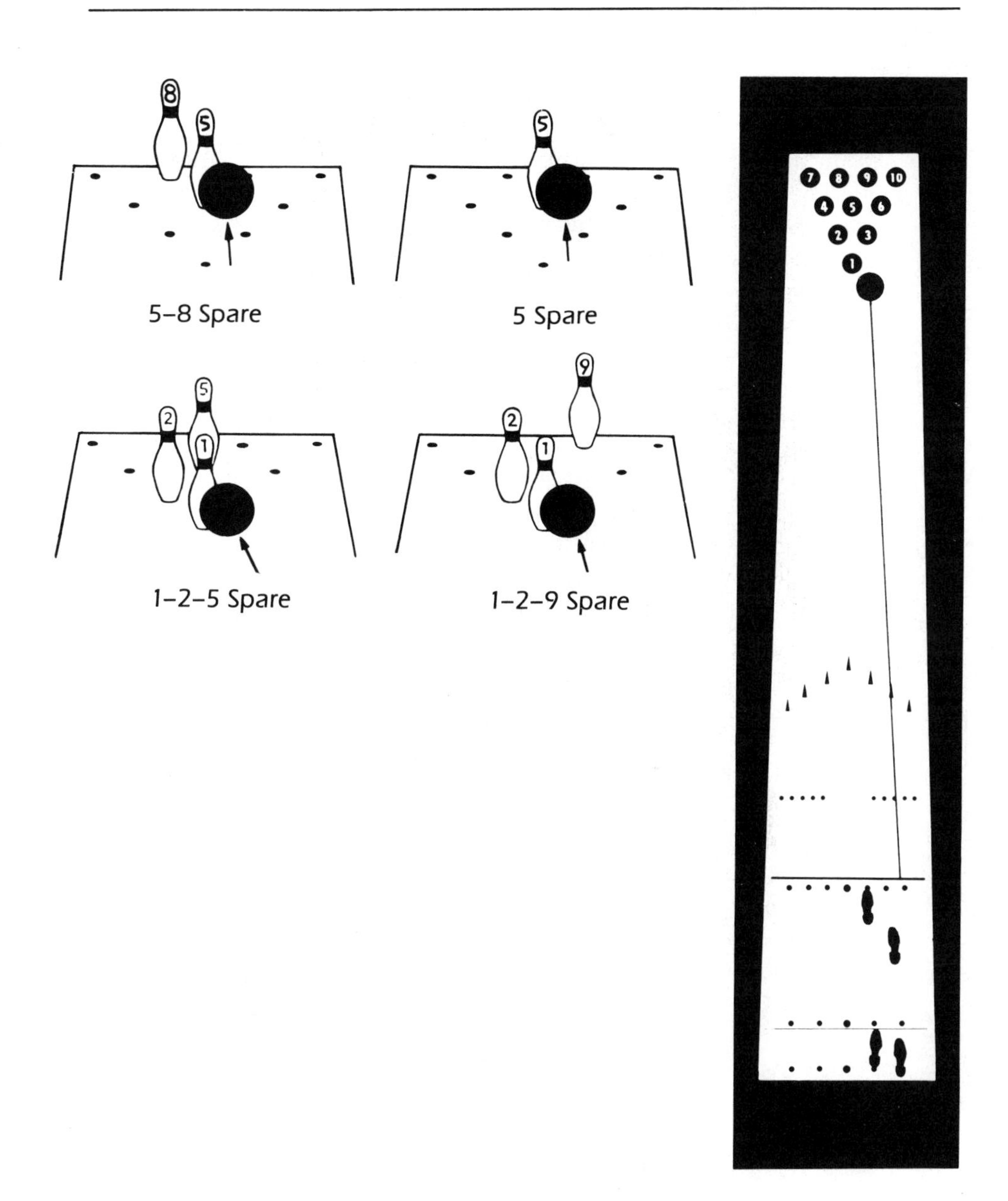

These middle spares can be picked up by using the strike ball

FIGURE 8-3

The 8 pin can be hit easily by moving one board right of your usual strike position on the approach area. By moving one board left of your strike position, the 9 pin can be picked up.

The 1–2–4–7 leave, or "fence," the 2 pin, and the 2–8 spare can be picked up by moving two boards to the right of your strike position (see Figure 8-4). Remember that in all of these middle spares, the spot to aim for is the second arrowhead from the right.

Next, let's look at the perimeter spares. These include the 7 pin, the 4 pin, the 4–7 spare, the 4–7–8 spare, the 2–7 split, the 7–8 spare, and the 2–4–7 spare on the left of the lane (see Figure 8-5). On the other side of the lane we can pick up the 10 pin, the 6 pin, the 6–10 spare, the 6–9–10 spare, the 3–10 split, the 9–10 spare, and the 3–6–10 spare (see Figure 8-6). Let's examine the 7-pin pickup first. Instead of taking your usual strike position, place your right foot on the outermost board of the lane proper. This is the black line in Figure 8-7. Now move four boards left of this position. This is an approximate starting place for a straight-ball bowler. (If your lane has seven dots in the approach area rather than five, as shown in Figure 8-7, your right foot will be on the first dot in from the right side of the lane.)

Hook-ball bowlers will have to move farther to the left. Your spot (both hook- and straight-ball bowlers) for this pickup and all other perimeter spares is the third arrowhead from the right side.of the alley. As you prepare to roll the ball, your feet should be pointed toward the third spot and in line with the 7 pin. If your ball goes over the spot but misses the pin, you need to adjust as you did for the strike ball. A miss on the right side of the pin calls for a move one board to the right. And a miss on the left side indicates a move one board to the left. Thus, you always move in the direction your ball was off.

A move of one board left from your 7-pin pickup position will enable you to pick up the 4 pin, the 4–7, the 4–7–8, the 2–4–7, and the 7–8 spares as well as the 2–7 split (see Figure 8-7).

For the 10-pin pickup, move to the left side of the approach area and place your left foot on the last board of the lane. Hook-ball bowlers can roll from this position, but if you

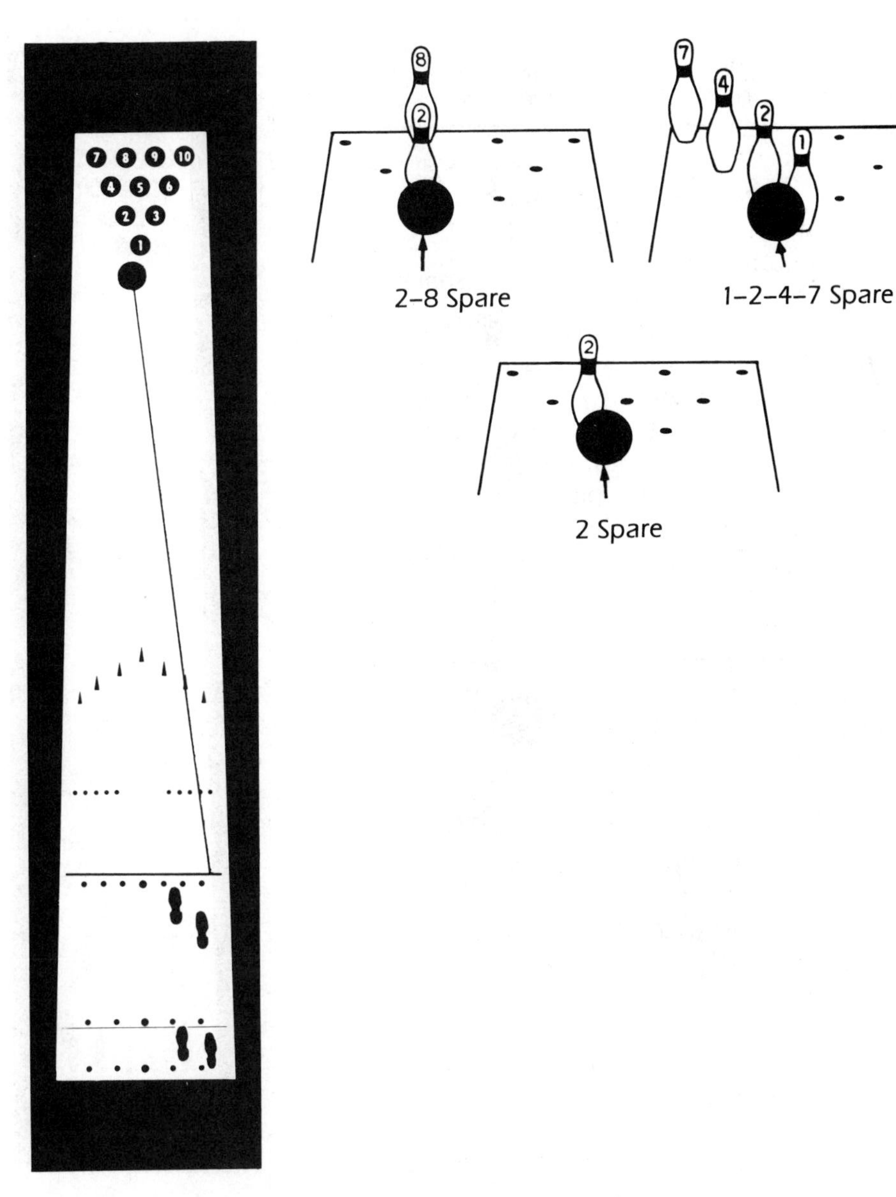

These spares can be picked up by moving two boards to the right of your strike position

FIGURE 8-4

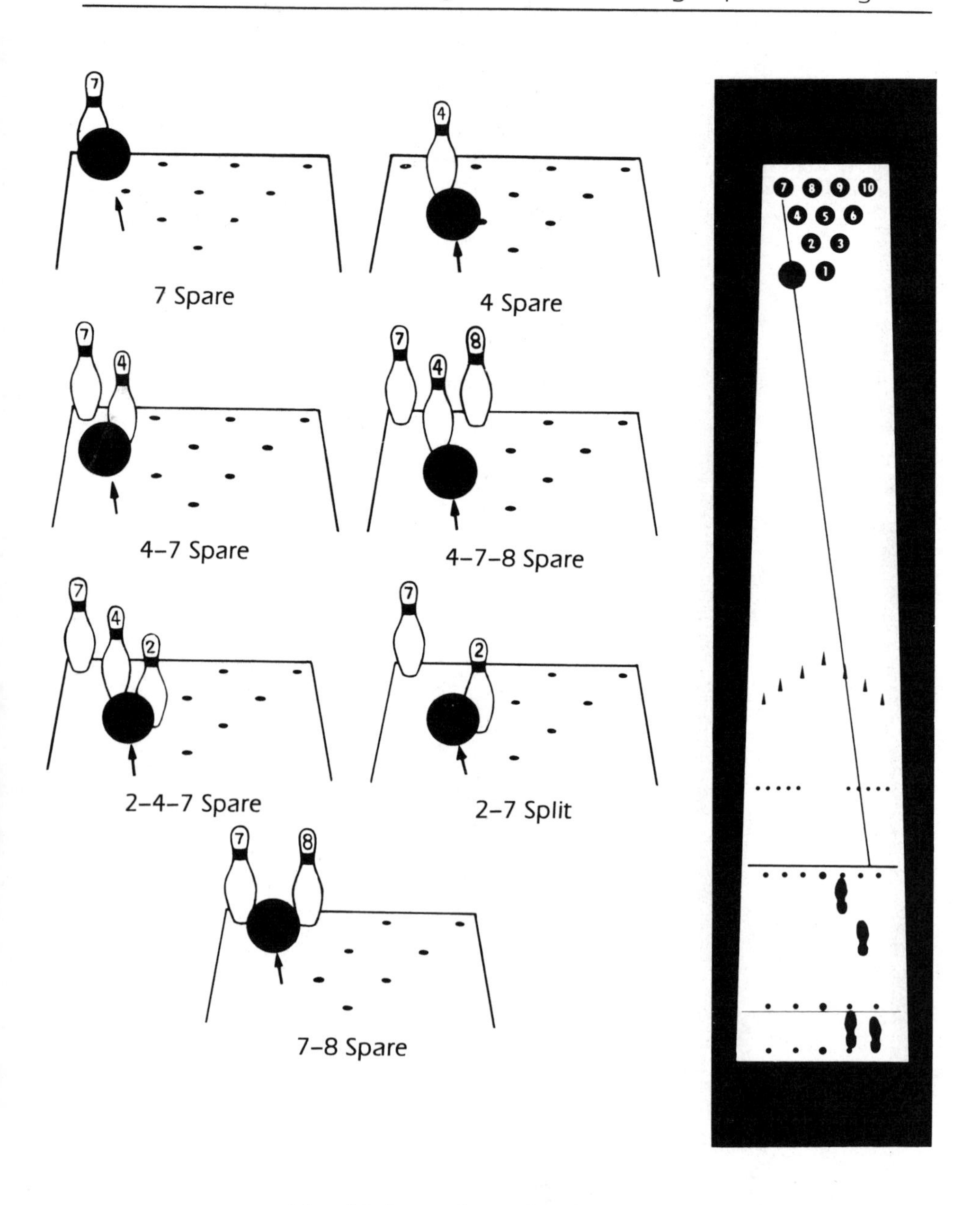

The third spot from the right is used for picking up these left-side spares

FIGURE 8-5

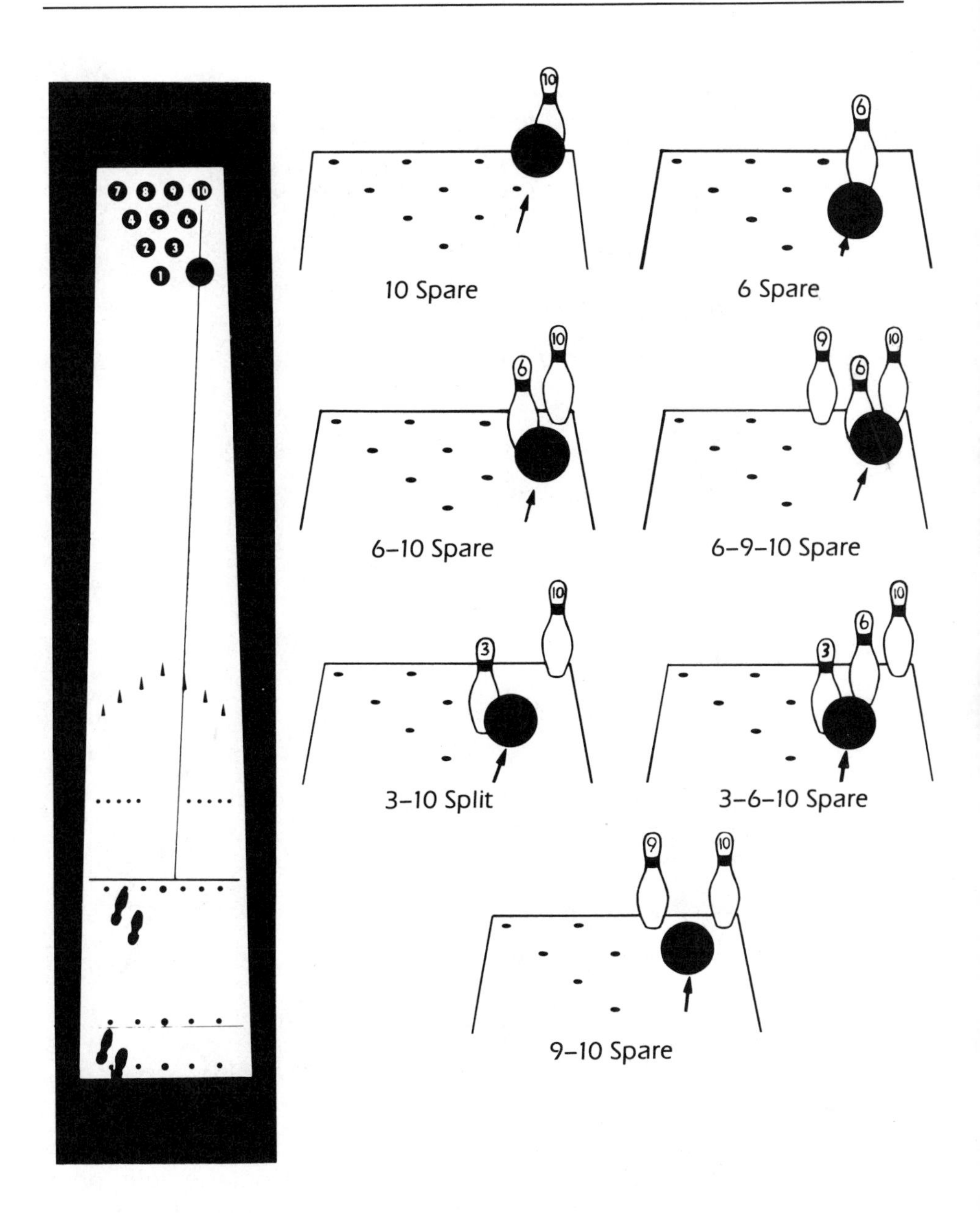

The third spot from the right is also used for picking up these right-side spares

FIGURE 8-6

FIGURE 8-7
FOOT POSITION FOR 7-PIN SPARE

roll a straight ball, move four boards to the right (see Figure 8-8). Again, sight over the same third spot from the right, point your toes in that direction, and roll the ball. If you hit the spot but miss the pin, make the necessary adjustment to determine your correct 10-pin position.

The 6 pin, the 6–10 , the 6–9–10, the 3–6–10, and the 9–

FIGURE 8-8
FOOT POSITION FOR 10-PIN SPARE

10 spares as well as the 3–10 split are picked up by moving one board right from your 10-pin position (see Figure 8-8).

These are not the only spares that can be picked up using spot bowling, but they are a good start. The five most frequent spares—as determined in a study conducted by the American Machine and Foundry Company—are all covered here. They are, in order of frequency, the 10, the 7, the 5, the 1–2–4, and the 6–10. By the time you have mastered the spares shown, you will probably be able to figure out other possibilities for yourself. For your convenience, a quick reference sheet for spot bowling follows. A tear-out version of the same sheet appears on page 93 of this book; a version for left-handers is on page 95.

QUICK REFERENCE SHEET FOR SPOT BOWLING

Strike Ball, 5–8 Spare, 1–2–5 Spare, 1–2–9 Spare

1. Place your right foot on the dot at the right side of the approach area.
2. Point toes toward 1–3 pocket.
3. Roll ball over the second spot from the right side of the lane. If you roll a hook, your starting position will be three or four boards to the left of the first dot.

Five Pin

1. Line up for strike ball.
2. Roll ball over second spot from the right. Hook-ball bowlers will have to move left one board from the strike position.

Two Pin, 1–2–4–7 Spare, 2–8 Spare

1. Move two boards to the right of your strike position.
2. Roll ball over the second spot from the right into 1–2 pocket.

Ten Pin

1. Place left foot on last board on the left side of the lane.
2. Move four boards to your right.

3. Point toes toward 10 pin.
4. Roll ball over third spot from the right side of the lane. If you roll a hook, start from the last board on the left side of the lane.

Six Pin, 6–10 Spare, 6–9–10 Spare, 3–6–10 Spare, 9–10 Spare, 3–10 Split

1. Move right one board from your position for the 10-pin pickup.
2. Roll ball over third spot from the right side of the lane.

Seven Pin

1. Place your right foot on the last board on the right side of the lane.
2. Move four boards to your left.
3. Point your toes at the 7 pin.
4. Roll ball over third spot from the right side of the lane. If you roll a hook, start eight boards from the right side of the lane.

Four Pin, 4–7 Spare, 4–7–8 Spare, 2–4–7 Spare, 7–8 Spare, 2–7 Split

1. Move left one board from your position for the 7-pin pickup.
2. Roll ball over third spot from the right side of the lane.

SPOT BOWLING CHECKSHEET

The spot bowling checksheet (Table 8-1) is designed to be used when you are practicing spare pickups or when you are actually rolling a game. The checksheet will help you become more consistent in hitting spots.

TABLE 8-1
SPOT BOWLING CHECKSHEET

	Right-Hander's Target	Left-Hander's Target
Strike ball	Second spot from right	Second spot from left
	△ △ △ △ △ ▲ △	△ ▲ △ △ △ △ △
10-pin pickup	Third spot from right	Third spot from left
	△ △ △ △ ▲ △ △	△ △ ▲ △ △ △ △
7-pin pickup	Third spot from right	Third spot from left
	△ △ △ △ ▲ △ △	△ △ ▲ △ △ △ △

Instructions: As you roll each frame, put an (X) to indicate where your ball rolled in relation to the targeted spot.

Example: △x △̽ x△

Strike Ball		10 Pin		7 Pin	
1.	△	1.	△	1.	△
2.	△	2.	△	2.	△
3.	△	3.	△	3.	△
4.	△	4.	△	4.	△
5.	△	5.	△	5.	△
6.	△	6.	△	6.	△
7.	△	7.	△	7.	△
8.	△	8.	△	8.	△
9.	△	9.	△	9.	△
10.	△	10.	△	10.	△

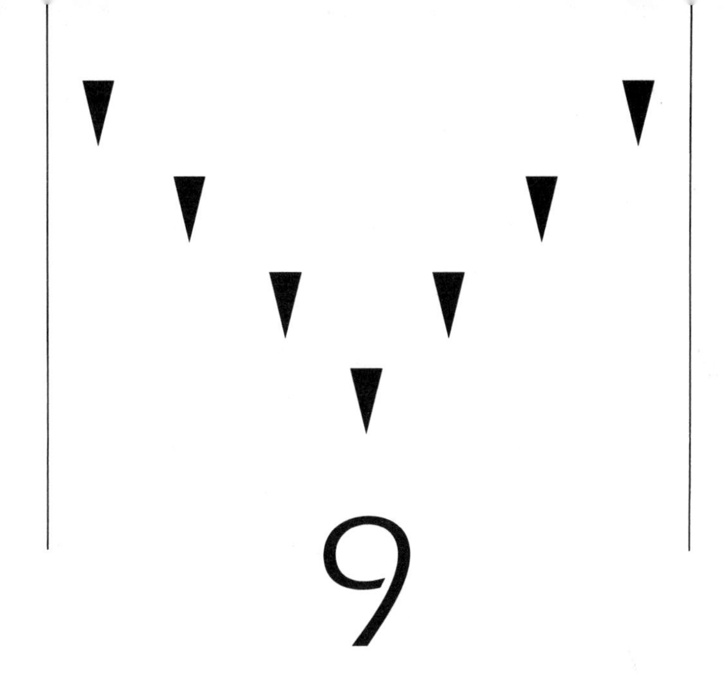

9

How to Keep Score

Scoring in bowling can appear quite complicated until you catch on to it. It will be helpful if you can keep these things in mind:

1. A game consists of ten frames, represented by the ten boxes on the scoresheet. You roll two balls in each frame unless you roll a strike with your first ball.
2. When you roll a strike, you get a score of 10 plus the number of pins toppled on the next two balls. You do not record your score for the strike frame until you have rolled the next two balls.
3. A spare is scored when you knock down all ten pins with two rolls. Your score for that frame is 10 plus the number of pins you knock down with the first ball in the next frame. You do not record your score for the frame in which you have made a spare until you have rolled your first ball in the next frame.
4. There is a system of symbols you must learn in scoring. These symbols help you to keep track of what is happening as you roll your game. They are also helpful in analyzing the strengths and weaknesses of your game.

The symbols used in scoring are presented here and are followed by a sample game.

SYMBOLS USED IN SCORING

Spare All pins are knocked down with two balls in a frame.

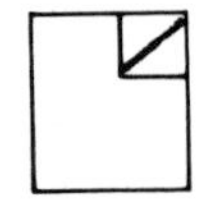

Strike All ten pins are knocked down with the first ball in a frame.

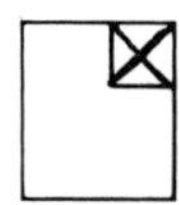

Miss (Error or Blow) Failure to bowl down all ten pins with two balls in a frame, except in the case of a split.

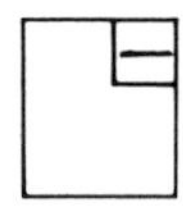

Split (Railroad) A leave in which the head pin is down and two or more pins remain standing with adjacent pins knocked down in front and between.

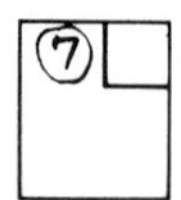

Converted Split A split that becomes a spare when the pins are picked up with the second ball in a frame.

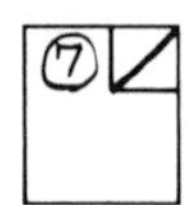

Some situations can arise that may make scoring a bit more difficult.

Foul on First Ball The bowler gets no score for the first ball and pins must be reracked for the second ball.

Foul on Second Ball No score is recorded for the second ball, so the total for the frame is the first ball count only.

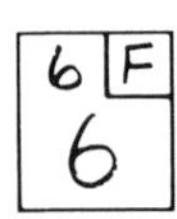

Recording Both Balls on Scoresheet In our scoring sample (see pages 55–57), only the score of the first ball is specially marked, though the score of the second ball may be calculated from this figure and the total. The method used in the scoring sample and the one that shows the score of both balls are shown here.

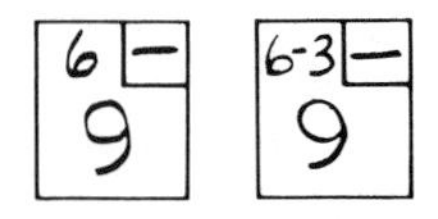

Strike Followed by Spare Score 20 for the strike frame since a strike gives 10 points plus the total of the next two balls.

Spare Followed by Strike Score 20 for the spare frame since a spare gives 10 points plus the score of the next ball.

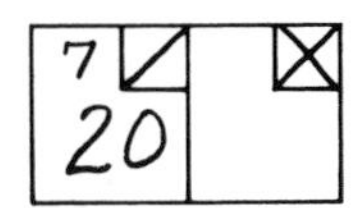

Double When you roll two strikes in succession, you must wait until you roll a third ball before posting a score in the first frame.

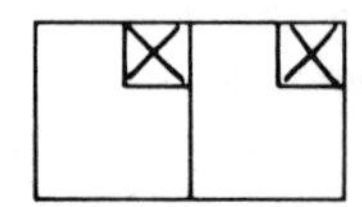

Turkey or Triple When you roll three strikes in succession, score 30 for the first strike frame. Thirty is the highest possible score for one frame.

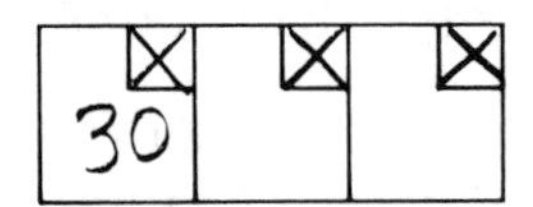

Strike Out A strike in the tenth frame followed by strikes with both bonus balls gives 30 points to the final frame. Thirty points is the highest score possible for the tenth frame.

8	9	10
8 –	5 –	X X X
130	135	165

Strike in the Tenth Frame Roll two extra balls to determine your score for the final frame.

8	9	10
8 –	X	X 6 3
130	156	175

Spare in the Tenth Frame Roll one extra ball to determine your score for the final frame.

8	9	10
8 –	7 –	9 / 7
130	137	154

SCORING A SAMPLE GAME

First Frame You roll two balls and knock down a total of seven pins, so you mark that number in the first frame and a (–) in the box to indicate the miss or error.

1	2	3	4	5	6	7	8	9	10
7 –									
7									

Second Frame On your first ball, you knock down all but the 7 and 10 pins. Circle the 8 to show the split. With your second ball you take out the 7 pin, giving you 9 for the frame and a total of 16 for the first two frames. Put 1 in the box to show you knocked down the 7 pin.

1	2	3	4	5	6	7	8	9	10
7 –	(8) 1								
7	16								

Third Frame This time you make your spare. Your first ball leaves only the 5 pin, and you knock it down with the second ball. Put a (/) in the box, but do not mark any score for the third frame. Having spared, your first ball's total in the next frame will be added to your score for the first three frames.

1	2	3	4	5	6	7	8	9	10
7 –	(8) 1	9 /							
7	16								

Fourth Frame You knock down seven pins with your first ball. Add 17 to your second frame total (10 for the spare plus 7 for the first ball in this frame) to get your third frame score. Your second ball knocks down two more pins but leaves one standing, so add 9 to your score and put a 2 in the box.

1	2	3	4	5	6	7	8	9	10
7 –	(8) 1	9 /	7 2						
7	16	33	42						

Fifth Frame Here, you register your first strike. Put the (X) in the box and wait for the next two rolls before you compute your score.

1	2	3	4	5	6	7	8	9	10
7 –	(8) 1	9 /	7 2	X					
7	16	33	42						

Sixth Frame Your first ball leaves a 3–10 split. Circle the 8 to show the split. Your second ball converts the split to a spare. Draw a (/) in the box to indicate this conversion. Add 20 to your fourth frame total (10 plus 8 plus 2) for your fifth frame total. Wait for your first ball in the seventh frame before computing your sixth frame total.

1	2	3	4	5	6	7	8	9	10
7 –	(8) 1	9 /	7 2	X	(8) /				
7	16	33	42	62					

Seventh Frame You score your second strike of the game. You put an (X) in the box and wait for your next two balls before figuring your total for this frame. Your sixth frame can now be recorded. Add 20 (10 plus 10) to your fifth frame total.

1	2	3	4	5	6	7	8	9	10
7 –	(8) 1	9 /	7 2	X	(8) /	X			
7	16	33	42	62	82				

Eighth Frame On your first ball you take down nine pins but fail to convert with the second ball. Put a (–) in the box to record the miss. Add 19 (10 plus 9) to the sixth frame total to get your seventh frame score. The nine pins are then added to the seventh frame total to complete the scoring in the eighth frame.

1	2	3	4	5	6	7	8	9	10
7 –	(8) 1	9 /	7 2	X	(8) /	X	9 –		
7	16	33	42	62	82	101	110		

Ninth Frame You strike again! This means you put an (X) in the box and wait till you roll your next two balls before you figure your ninth frame total.

1	2	3	4	5	6	7	8	9	10
7 –	(8) /	9 /	7 2	X	(8) /	X	9 –	X	
7	16	33	42	62	82	101	110		

Tenth Frame Your ball goes right in the pocket and you roll another strike. That gives you two more rolls. With the first of the next two rolls, you knock down eight pins. This adds 28 to your eighth frame total (10 plus 10 plus 8). With your next and final ball, you pick up the remaining two pins. This means you add 20 (10 plus 8 plus 2) for the tenth frame. Your total score for the game is 158.

1	2	3	4	5	6	7	8	9	10
7 –	(8) /	9 /	7 2	X	(8) /	X	9 –	X	X 8 /
7	16	33	42	62	82	101	110	138	158

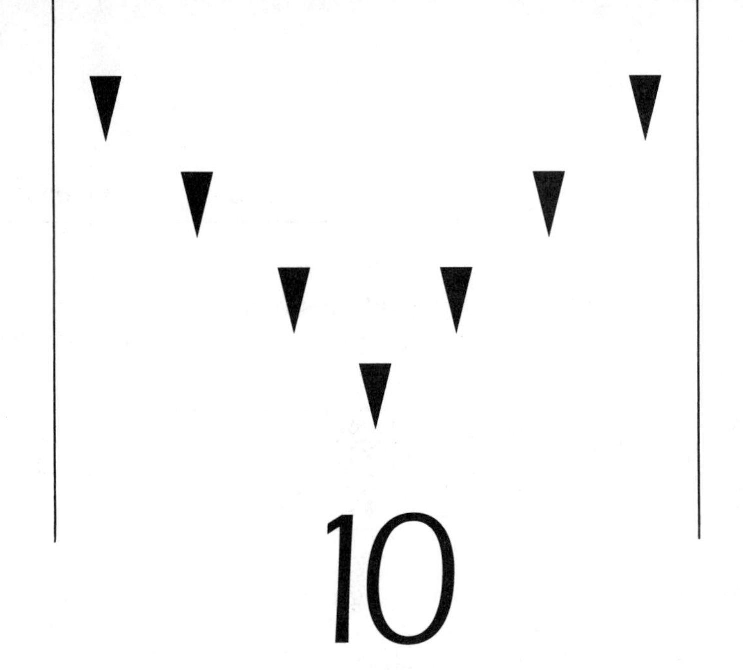

10

Selection and Care of Bowling Equipment

As in any other sport, the proper equipment can make a difference in your success. It is difficult, if not impossible, to be a consistent bowler using a house ball. You won't get the proper fit very often. You need to have a ball that gives you confidence. Having your own ball properly fitted and drilled can give you that positive feeling.

Having comfortable shoes can also add to your bowling skill. For the best quality in shoes and balls, pro shops and bowling supply stores are better sources of equipment than department stores. Your decision will depend, of course, on how serious you are about bowling and how much money you have to spend.

BOWLING BALLS

Weight

There are a number of factors to be considered in selecting a bowling ball. One factor is weight. The general principle is that you should use the heaviest ball you can control. The heavier ball will give you better pin action. Women used to be advised to use a 12- to 14-pound ball, but today many women can handle a 15- or 16-pound ball.

Again, your feelings about your ability to handle the heavy ball are to be considered. It is suggested that you practice with a heavier ball before you decide to purchase one.

Grip

Beginning bowlers would probably be more comfortable with the conventional grip than with fingertip or semifingertip. (See page 79.) When you move past the beginner's stage and develop consistency in your delivery, a move to the semifingertip ball will improve your pin action, and your strike production should go up.

Plastic or Rubber Ball?

The modern plastic ball is considered superior to the rubber ball. The plastic ball creates more friction in contact with the lane and results in a greater hook and pin-carrying action.

SHOES

The sole of the sliding foot (left foot for right-handed bowlers) is made of leather or Teflon. The nonsliding shoe has a sole of plastic or rubber. The best-made shoes will have the sole stitched to the uppers rather than glued. Well-fitted shoes should feel comfortable when you first put them on and require little breaking in. If you're using the bowling lanes' shoes, check the soles to see if they're for right-handed or left-handed bowlers.

Finally, try to match your equipment needs to your level of bowling skill and interest. If possible, have a bowling pro observe you bowl and get his or her suggestions for the type of ball best suited to your bowling style. Ask the veteran low-handicap bowlers in your community about what shoes and bowling bags they recommend.

GLOVES

For bowlers who feel they need wrist support, a glove can be helpful. Make sure the glove you purchase has metal strips on both the back and the front of the glove. The metal helps you maintain a stable wrist position. The metal should be removable so you can wash your glove before it gets smelly like an old shoe.

CARE OF EQUIPMENT

It is important to keep your bowling ball clean and avoid scratching it. A plastic bag cover is recommended for avoiding wear and tear on the ball when you have it in your bowling bag. The use of foot powder will prolong the life of your bowling shoes and may make you a more acceptable bowling companion. Airing out your shoes rather than keeping them in the zipped bag all the time is a good idea.

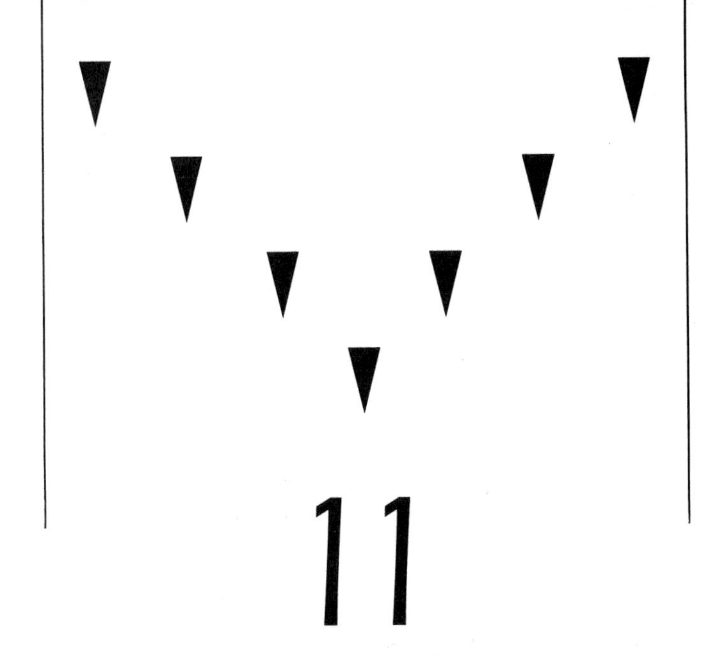

11

Bowling Rules: A Synopsis

Official bowling competition in the United States is conducted under the auspices of the ABC and the WIBC. For all of its league and tournament competition, the WIBC adopted the ABC rules. The following summarizes the most significant official rules and regulations as established by the ABC.

1. The overall length of a bowling lane shall be 62 feet, 10-3/16 inches from foul line to pit edge. It must be 60 feet from the foul line to the center of the 1-pin spot. The width of the lane must not exceed 42 inches or be less than 41 inches. A diagram of a lane is shown in Figure 11-1.
2. Approved pins shall be made of sound, hard maple. Pins constructed of material other than wood, such as synthetic material or plastic-coated wood, may be used but must comply with ABC specifications. The weight of the standard wood pin must not exceed 3 pounds, 10

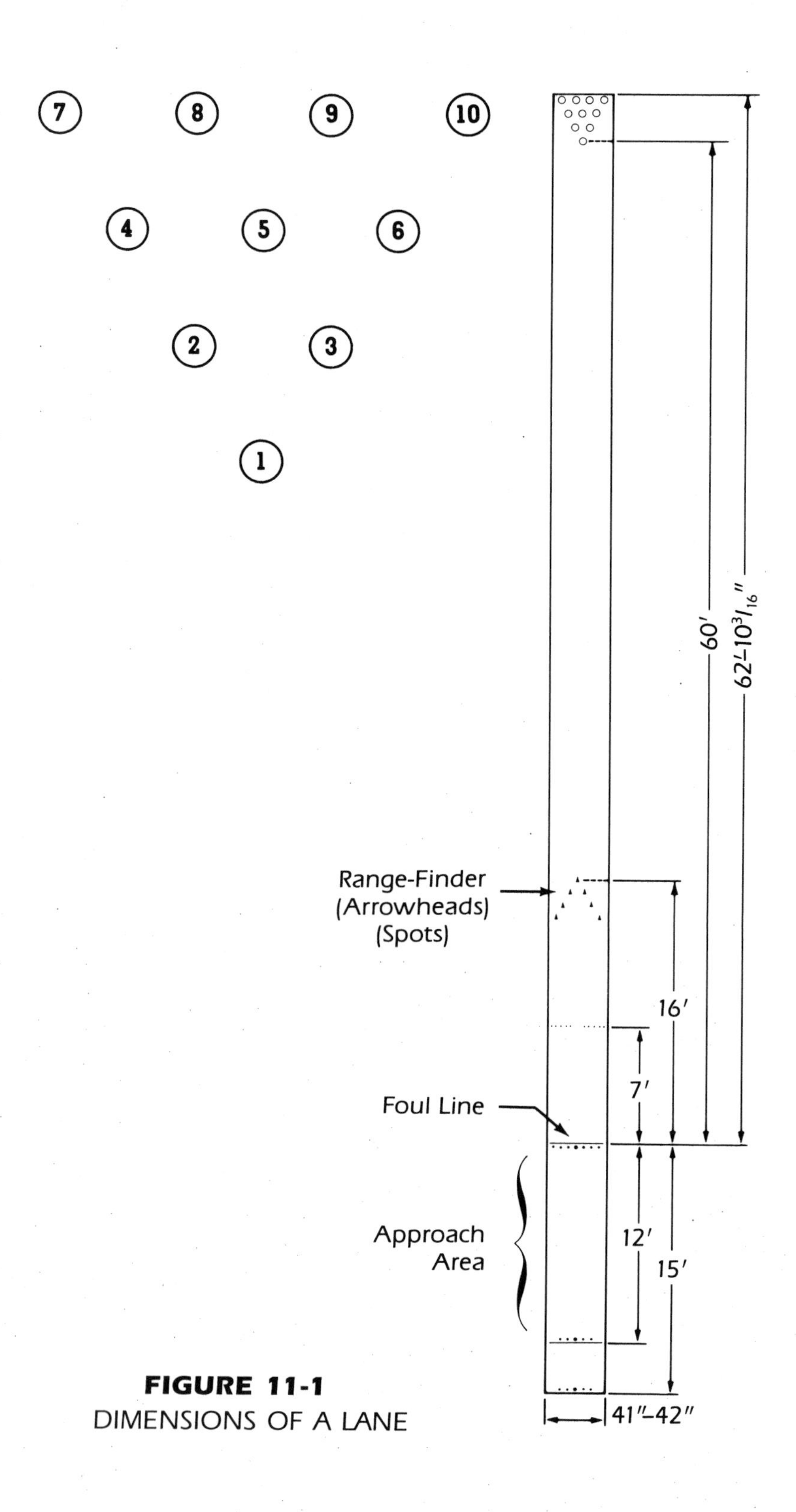

FIGURE 11-1
DIMENSIONS OF A LANE

ounces, or be less than 3 pounds, 2 ounces. The height of pins must be 15 inches.

3. Bowling balls shall not exceed 27 inches in circumference. Figure 11-2 shows a pin and ball. The ball must weigh no more than 16 pounds.
4. Pins that are knocked down by a ball that first entered the gutter do not count.
5. Pins that bounce off the lane, rebound, and remain standing are considered pins standing.
6. If the bowler or any part of his or her body touches or goes beyond the foul line and touches any part of the bowling lane during or after delivery, it is a foul. Touching a wall, post, division board, or any other

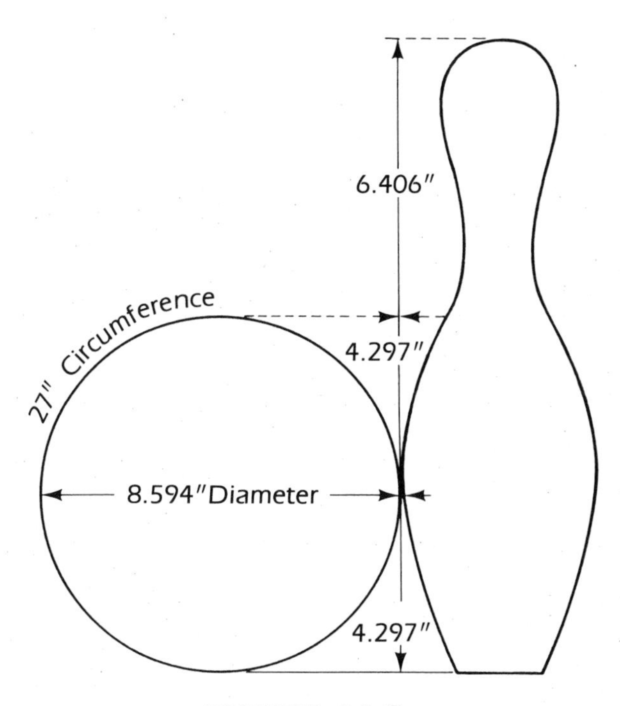

FIGURE 11-2
POSITION OF PINS AND SIZE OF BALL

structure beyond the foul line constitutes a foul. Walls adjacent to end lanes should have a vertical foul line.

7. A foul ball counts as a ball rolled, but the pins that are knocked down do not count. After the pins are reset, the bowler is allowed to roll her or his second ball. If she or he knocks all the pins down, a spare, not a strike, is given.
8. If a bowler fouls on the second ball, the pins knocked down with that ball do not count. The pins knocked down with the first ball do count.
9. If a bowler fouls on both his or her first and second ball in a frame, the score for that frame is zero.
10. A ball is declared "dead," the pins are reset, and the bowler must roll again if
    a. One or more pins were missing from the setup.
    b. The ball comes in contact with any foreign object.
    c. A human pinsetter removes or interferes with any pin before the ball stops rolling or before it reaches the pins.
    d. A bowler is interfered with while making his delivery, providing he calls attention to this fact before the ball reaches the pins.

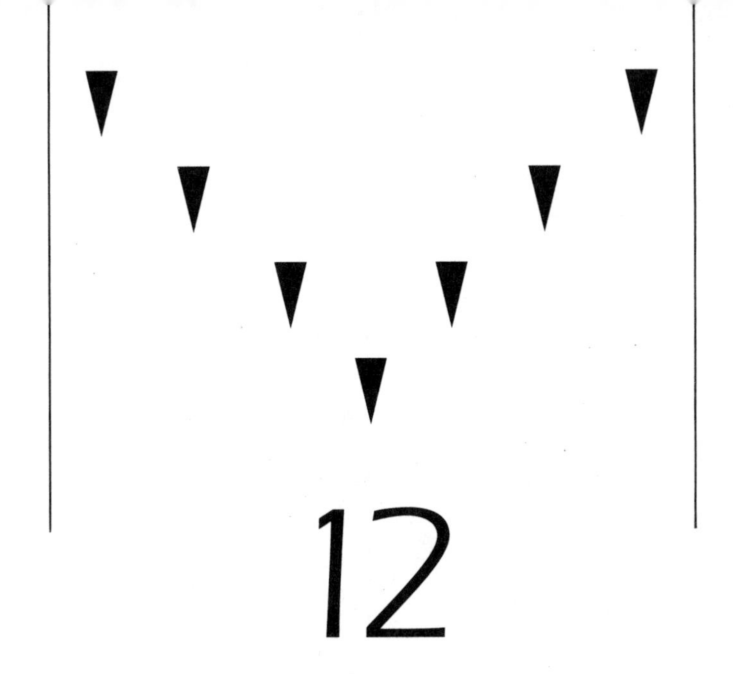

12

Bowling in Competition

No matter how casual your interest in bowling may be when you first learn the game, the challenge of bettering your previous efforts will grow. As your skill improves, you are likely to develop a real zest for competition. Many bowlers find the excitement of competing against others the most satisfying experience of the sport.

HANDICAP LEAGUES

For regular bowling competition, most people join a group at their local bowling establishment and bowl on a five-person team in an organized league. The use of handicaps enables bowlers of different abilities to roll in the same league. There are various ways of computing handicaps, and two systems are presented here. The first one is for beginning bowlers (Table 12-1); the second is for intermediate or advanced bowlers (Table 12-2). In either case, a bowler with a 180 average is referred to as a scratch bowler, or a bowler who does not have any handicap.

TABLE 12-1
HANDICAPS FOR BEGINNERS

A H	A H	A H	A H	A H	A H
60–108	80–90	100–72	120–54	140–36	160–18
61–107	81–89	101–71	121–53	141–35	161–17
62–106	82–88	102–70	122–52	142–34	162–16
63–105	83–87	103–69	123–51	143–33	163–15
64–104	84–86	104–68	124–50	144–32	164–14
65–103	85–85	105–67	125–49	145–31	165–13
66–102	86–84	106–66	126–48	146–30	166–12
67–101	87–83	107–65	127–47	147–29	167–11
68–100	88–82	108–64	128–46	148–28	168–10
69–99	89–81	109–63	129–45	149–27	169–9
70–99	90–81	110–63	130–45	150–27	170–9
71–98	91–80	111–62	131–44	151–26	171–8
72–97	92–79	112–61	132–43	152–25	172–7
73–96	93–78	113–60	133–42	153–24	173–6
74–95	94–77	114–59	134–41	154–23	174–5
75–94	95–76	115–58	135–40	155–22	175–4
76–93	96–75	116–57	136–39	156–21	176–3
77–92	97–74	117–56	137–38	157–20	177–2
78–91	98–73	118–55	138–37	158–19	178–1
79–90	99–72	119–54	139–36	159–18	179–0
					180–0

Note: The table gives the corresponding handicap (H) for a person's average (A) between 60 and 180. The handicap represents 90 percent of the difference between each average and 180. Any person with an average of 180 or over receives no handicap.

LEAGUE COMPETITION

Figure 12-1 provides a scoresheet for a typical handicap league. Note how Westley, leadoff person of the Hilltoppers, is a key in the Hilltoppers' victory. Going into the game, Westley carried a 104 average, which rated a handicap of 57. The 137 game coupled with the handicap of 57 gave Westley a total of 194. This was good enough to beat Hill, the best bowler on the Whirlwinds. Hill, the opponent's anchor person, carried a 171 average and a handicap of 7. Hill rolled a very

TABLE 12-2

HANDICAPS FOR INTERMEDIATE AND ADVANCED BOWLERS

A H	A H	A H	A H	A H	A H
55–94	76–78	97–62	118–47	139–31	160–15
56–93	77–77	98–62	119–46	140–30	161–14
57–92	78–77	99–61	120–45	141–29	162–14
58–92	79–76	100–60	121–44	142–29	163–13
59–91	80–75	101–59	122–44	143–28	164–12
60–90	81–74	102–59	123–43	144–27	165–11
61–89	82–74	103–58	124–42	145–26	166–11
62–89	83–73	104–57	125–41	146–26	167–10
63–88	84–72	105–56	126–41	147–25	168–9
64–87	85–71	106–56	127–40	148–24	169–8
65–86	86–71	107–55	128–39	149–23	170–8
66–86	87–70	108–54	129–38	150–23	171–7
67–85	88–69	109–53	130–38	151–22	172–6
68–84	89–68	110–53	131–37	152–21	173–5
69–83	90–68	111–52	132–36	153–20	174–5
70–83	91–67	112–51	133–35	154–20	175–4
71–82	92–66	113–50	134–35	155–19	176–3
72–81	93–65	114–50	135–34	156–18	177–2
73–80	94–65	115–49	136–33	157–17	178–2
74–80	95–64	116–48	137–32	158–17	179–1
75–79	96–63	117–47	138–32	159–16	180–0

Note: The table gives the handicap (H) for any person's average (A) between 55 and 180. The handicap represents 75 percent of the difference between each average and 180; a person with an average of 180 or more receives no handicap.

respectable 160 but a handicap of 7, added to her score, gave a total of 167, twenty-seven pins less than Westley's total. This illustrates how the handicap system enables all bowlers to compete on an equal basis regardless of the difference in their abilities.

A running account of the match, from frame to frame, was kept by totaling cumulative marks (strikes or spares) as the game progressed (see the numbers divided by diagonal lines at the center of the scoresheet). This is an unofficial way to keep track of how one team is doing in competition with another. It is an approximate measure, but it makes the game

TEAMS HILLTOPPERS VS WHIRLWINDS

	PLAYER	HDCP	1	2	3	4	5	6	7	8	9	10	TOTAL
1	Westley	57	9 - 9	8 - 17	X 37	5 / 55	8 - 63	9 - 72	4 / 91	9 / 110	9 / 128	8 / - 137	137
2	Valerio	43	9 - 9	G 9 18	7 ② 27	6 / 46	9 / 65	9 - 74	X 94	7 / 109	5 / 126	7 2 135	135
3	Lee	0	8 / 20	X 40	9 / 57	7 / 77	X 97	9 / 117	X 137	9 / 151	4 / 171	X X X 201	201
4	Johnson	0	6 3 9	X 29	9 / 47	8 1 56	7 / 73	7 ② 82	7 2 91	6 3 100	5 4 109	X X 8 137	137
5	TOTAL	100											610 +100 710
MARKS	Hilltoppers Whirlwinds	⑤	1 / 6	3 / 10	6 / 12	9 / 13	12 / 14	13 / 17	16 / 19	19 / 20	22 / 21	28 / 24	
8	Tucker	57	7 1 8	9 / 25	7 / 41	6 2 49	8 - 57	X 75	8 - 83	7 2 92	8 ① 101	X 9 - 120	120
9	O'Brien	45	5 4 9	7 / 25	6 - 31	9 - 40	9 - 49	8 / 68	9 - 77	9 - 86	X 112	X 6 / 132	132
10	Butler	41	1 - 1	4 / 21	X - 41	8 / 54	3 4 61	7 1 69	8 / 82	3 5 90	1 8 99	6 - 105	105
11	Hill	7	X - 20	7 / 37	7 ② 46	8 1 55	9 / 74	9 / 94	X 114	3 / 133	9 - 142	X 7 1 160	160
12	TOTAL	150											517 +150 667

FIGURE 12-1
SAMPLE SCORESHEET
FOR A HANDICAP LEAGUE

more exciting because you don't have to wait until the end to see who is winning. At the beginning of the game each team captain adds up the handicaps for his or her team. The Hilltoppers had a total of 100, while the Whirlwinds had a team handicap of 150. Since each bowler's handicap is determined by his or her current average, the team with the smaller handicap, the Hilltoppers, would be the better overall bowlers. However, the Hilltoppers *have* to bowl better than the Whirlwinds to win because of the fifty-pin difference in the two teams' handicaps. To indicate this difference at the start of the game, the Whirlwinds were given 5 marks (indicated by the number in the circle). Each mark represents ten pins, and thus the 5 marks represent the fifty-pin difference in team handicaps.

The Hilltoppers did not overtake their opponents until the ninth frame. A triple (three consecutive strikes) by Lee in the last frame really helped provide the margin of victory.

TOURNAMENTS

For those who seek more difficult tests of their bowling skills, there are numerous bowling tournaments conducted at the state, regional, and national levels. The most prominent tournaments are the annual ABC and WIBC championships.

The ABC championship is conducted in the following categories:

1. Classic Division, for professional bowlers who average 190 or more.
2. Regular Division, for outstanding bowlers who are not professionals.
3. Booster Division, for five ABC members none of whom are identified as professionals. The combined averages of a team in this division shall not exceed 850.

In the Classic and Regular Divisions, competition is conducted for five-person teams, doubles (two-person teams), singles (individual bowlers), and all events. All events contenders must participate in team, doubles, and singles competition.

The WIBC championships are held in the following categories:

1. Open Division, for bowlers with averages of 171 and over.
2. Division I, for bowlers with averages of 151 through 170.
3. Division II, for bowlers with averages of 150 and under.

Competition is held for teams, doubles, singles, and all events.

College students will be interested in the intercollegiate bowling championships. The National Bowling Council (NBC) Intercollegiate Bowling Championships (IBC) have been held annually, starting in 1975. Since bowling is not a National Collegiate Athletic Association (NCAA) sport, most of the participants are members of independent club sports teams rather than varsity sports teams. The tournament format consists of twenty-four teams, twelve men's and twelve women's. A team consists of five players. Teams are determined by sectional roll-off competition. The winning men's and women's teams from the National Junior College Athletic Association championships also earn a berth to the IBC.

The IBC features not only five-player team bowling but also a very unique type of bowling competition called the Baker System or single-line scoring. The Baker System involves each member of the team. The first player rolls frames one and five, the second player rolls frames two and six. The third player rolls three and seven, the fourth player four and eight. The anchor bowler rolls the fifth and tenth frames. In the finals, each team rolls two games with the largest team total determining the winner.

In an effort to increase bowling participation among college students, the Young American Bowling Alliance (YABA) introduced a new program, the Campus Bowling Program, during the 1989–90 season.

The Campus Program gives recreational bowlers a chance to compete in league, intramural, and physical education activities. The result of this program was a significant jump in collegiate bowling participation. During its first year the Campus Program signed up nearly eighteen thousand students. The fee for the program is a one-time participation fee of one hundred dollars for each school. There is no individual bowler fee. For the blanket fee, each campus can sign up an unlimited number of bowlers. With the membership, each campus is provided with Campus Bowling Awards. The Campus Program has an unusual awards system. Instead of trophies the program provides pens, notebooks, bowling towels, mugs, and key chains. The emphasis is on giving instant recognition to stimulate student interest in bowling. During the first year of the Campus Bowling Program, each school involved in this program reported over three hundred participants. The colleges with the most participants were the University of Wisconsin-Eau Claire, Illinois State University, and Mankato State University, Minnesota, with over thirteen hundred students on each campus.

SPECIAL EVENTS

As a change of pace from the usual league-type bowling competition, there are a number of special events that can add fun to your bowling experience. They can be adapted to singles, doubles, team, mixed competition, or almost any combination of these, and endless variations can be made in the rules to suit your situation. Most of the events described here are included through the courtesy of the National Bowling Council, 1919 Pennsylvania Avenue N.W., Washington, D.C. 20006.

Beat the Champ (NBC)

Announce a beat-the-champ tournament. The champ can be the top intramural bowler of your college or the winner of an all-campus tournament. Ask the champ to roll a target score and then have those who entered the competition try to beat this score. The tournament can also start with the contestants rolling a single game or a three-game series; then the champ can roll his or her games.

Blind Bowling

Hang a wire with a curtain about halfway down the lane to block the bowler's view of the pins. With automatic pin machines showing the pins remaining, regular scoring can be used. This is excellent practice for spot bowling.

Best Ball (NBC)

A doubles team competition is just right for a best ball event. The partners bowl on adjacent lanes. The first player on each team rolls the first ball. If that player scores a strike, that team has a strike in the first frame. If that player fails to make a strike, his or her partner tries for the strike. If neither strikes, each tries to make a spare. The highest count of either team member is the team score for that frame.

Variations include two lower-average bowlers competing against a single higher-average bowler. Their two chances at a strike or spare provide the necessary handicap to make the match interesting.

Head Pin

Each bowler rolls only one ball per frame. The score for that frame is the number of pins knocked down, providing the head pin goes down. If the head pin is missed, the score for that frame is zero. Twelve balls are allowed, and a perfect game is twelve strikes or 120 points.

Free-Strike Tournaments (NBC)

Free-strike tournaments offer many variations. A free strike can be given in the first frame. The first ball in the tenth frame is also a great free-strike spot. Another possibility is that a series of free strikes can be awarded for the strategic third, sixth, and ninth frames. Each bowler automatically receives these strikes in the predetermined frame or frames. They are recorded on the scoresheet, and then the bowlers roll their regular game. The games are over quickly, and the scores are really high—great confidence builders. It is not unusual for bowlers to conveniently avoid mentioning the free strikes when they report their scores to friends.

Golf Bowling (NBC)

The low-score idea is used in this event. Each bowler rolls ten frames. A strike counts as 1, a spare counts as 2, and if any pins are standing after the second ball, the bowlers receive a score of 3. The lowest score possible is 10; the highest, 30.

Scotch Doubles (NBC)

In this type of doubles play one partner rolls the first ball, and his or her partner rolls the second. The partners continue alternate rolling throughout the game.

Wild Strike (NBC)

In the wild-strike tournament each bowler rolls a single game in the usual fashion, but after the game is completed, he or she is allowed to replace any frame with a strike.

SPECIAL EVENTS FOR SPECIAL PEOPLE

Bowling is a sport in which a wide variety of people can participate. Young children, senior citizens, and the physically and mentally handicapped can all enjoy bowling.

As your skill and knowledge move up the scale, you may want to help some of these special people experience the fun of bowling. You could become a teacher-coach in the Young American Bowling Alliance league in your community. Bowling competition for handicapped children through the Special Olympics might be a program of interest to you. Or you might want to volunteer as a bowling instructor for a program offered by your local senior citizens center. Some bowling establishments provide special railings that enable blind persons to bowl. You could become involved in a community project to help purchase such equipment.

Your bowling instructor can provide you with information about these programs. Get involved; you'll be glad you did.

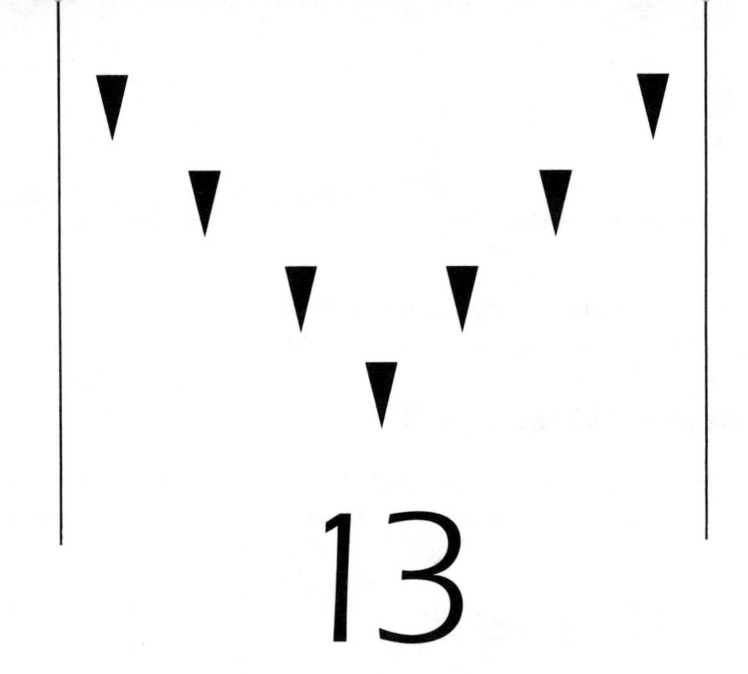

13

Advanced Techniques: The Hook Ball

The average score for men who bowl in a league is 159; the average for women is 132. If your average is much below these figures, you probably need to continue practicing your basic skills, which include learning how to roll a hook ball. As you begin to move above these averages, you can begin to examine the type of ball you are throwing.

What really happens when a bowler makes a strike? Why is a hook ball considered better than a straight ball, and what is a full-roller? When you get curious about the answers to these questions, you are probably moving beyond the beginning stage and are getting ready for more advanced information and play. Keep in mind, however, that skilled performers in any sport keep working to perfect the basic techniques. Smoothness, rhythm, balance, follow-through, and consistency will remain important skills for you to master completely.

But let's move ahead to what can make you a more accomplished bowler, now that you are acquainted with the basics.

MAKING THE PERFECT STRIKE

Why is the hook ball more effective than the straight ball in producing strikes? The answer lies in the angle at which the hook ball contacts the 1 or head pin. Figure 13-1 shows a perfect strike in which the ball first goes into the 1–3 pocket. There it topples the 1 pin, which then knocks over the 2, 4, and 7 pins, in domino fashion. When the ball hits the 1 pin, the ball is deflected and hits the 3 pin. The 3 pin then pushes into the 6 pin, which takes out the 10 pin. The ball meanwhile continues on its way, knocking out the 5 and 9 pins. Then the 5 pin is pushed into the 8 pin by the ball's action, and you have made yourself a perfect strike. Note that there are four points at which the ball contacts pins—at the 1, 3, 5, and 9 pins. For a strike to happen, the ball has to hit the 1 pin exactly at the center of the 1–2–4–7 line (see Figure 13-1).

The hook ball, which curves to the left as it comes into the 1–3 pocket, approaches the 1 pin on the 1–2–4–7 centerline more directly head on than a straight ball does. This enhances the possibility of starting off the correct sequence of events that make for a strike.

FULL-ROLLER, SEMIROLLER, AND SPINNER

There are three basic types of hook balls: the full-roller, the semiroller, and the spinner. All three are rolled with either the thumb at ten o'clock and ring finger at four o'clock or the thumb at eleven o'clock and ring finger at five o'clock. The difference between these three rolls occurs in the release.

The next time you bowl, look at your ball after you have rolled a few times. The accumulation of oil and dust from the lanes will make a ring around your ball (see Figure 13-2). You are most apt to see this ring between the thumbhole and the finger holes, circling the middle of the ball. This indicates a full-roller and is the easiest roll for the average or slightly above average bowler because the ball is released with a straight lifting action and little or no turn of the hand. Some

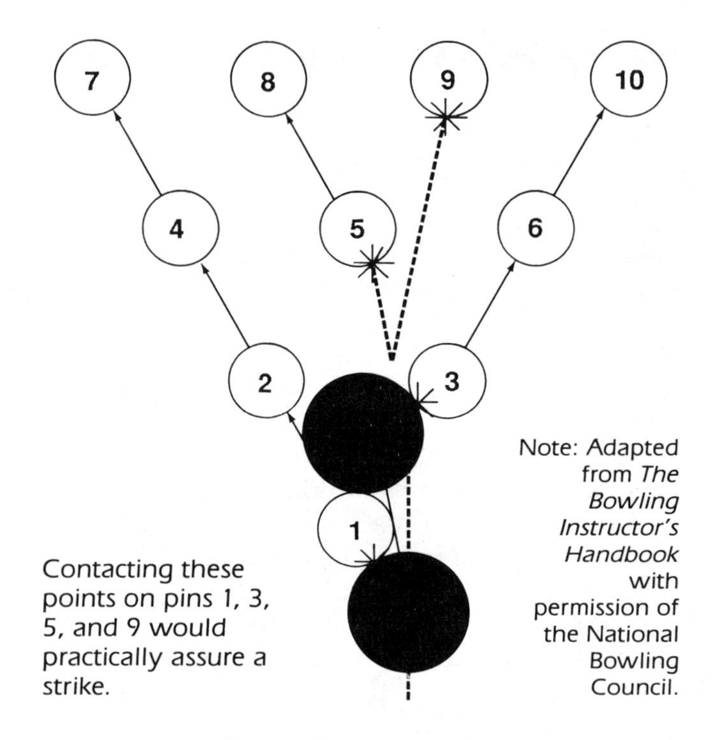

FIGURE 13-1
CONTACT POINTS FOR A PERFECT STRIKE

bowling experts, however, maintain that there is a slight turn of the thumbhole in a clockwise manner from ten toward eleven o'clock with the full-roller. This occurs as the ball is lifted with the fingers at the point of release.

The semiroller has the ring below the center of the ball. To roll this type of hook ball, keep the wrist straight and the thumb turned in a counterclockwise direction from ten to nine o'clock as the ball is lifted with the fingers. The semiroller is more difficult to master, but it does make the ball hook more sharply, and drives it into the 1–2–4–7 pins at the best angle for a strike.

The spinner has the ring even lower than the semiroller and is generally not recommended for most bowlers because

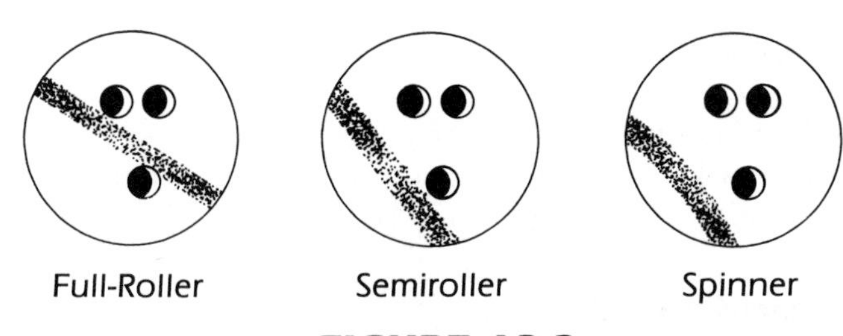

FIGURE 13-2
DUST LINES ON THE THREE TYPES OF ROLLS

it requires unusual wrist action. The counterclockwise turn of the hand at release is quite pronounced and requires a delicate touch to perfect.

VARIABLES THAT AFFECT THE HOOK

If your hook ball is to be effective and consistent, you should be aware of the variables that affect the amount your ball hooks.

To make a change in the type of hook ball you roll using one of the variables mentioned here, firmly establish the new technique through practice. Don't attempt to do it while bowling in competition. Practice does indeed make perfect.

Hand Position

If your thumb is at eleven o'clock and your ring finger is at five o'clock, your ball will have a slight hook, If your thumb is at ten o'clock and ring finger is at four o'clock, you will get more hooking action. The rotation of your hand in a counterclockwise manner, as in the semiroller, exaggerates the hook even more. Whatever hand position you use, be aware that your delivery may vary somewhat from day to day. Practice is important. It's what keeps this day-to-day variation to a minimum.

Ball Speed

By decreasing the speed of your ball, you can increase the amount of hook. To reduce hook, increase the ball speed. Tips for changing the speed of your ball are listed on page 22.

Lane Conditions

The amount of dressing or lane oil on the lanes definitely affects the amount of hook. The more dressing, the less the ball will hook because of reduced friction. The oil causes your ball to skid more, and so rotation is reduced.

Ball Position at Release

If you release your ball right at the foul line rather than some distance beyond the foul line, your ball will have further to travel to get to the pins, so your ball will begin to lose some rotation, which results in a lessened hook. That is why it is recommended that you release your ball 15 to 18 inches beyond the foul line for best hooking action. Remember, though, not to touch anything on the lane beyond the foul line.

Wrist Position

If your hand is bent slightly forward, rather than having your wrist straight at release, the hook will be exaggerated. A straight wrist helps you develop a consistent hook.

Lift

Lift is the upward pressure applied by the fingers to the ball at the moment of release. The more lift you apply, the more your ball hooks. To be most effective, the lift should be applied by your fingers after your thumb clears the thumbhole. The force for the lift is increased if you bend your arm upward at the elbow at the moment of release. If you follow through until your thumb reaches shoulder height, you will ensure the proper elbow bend.

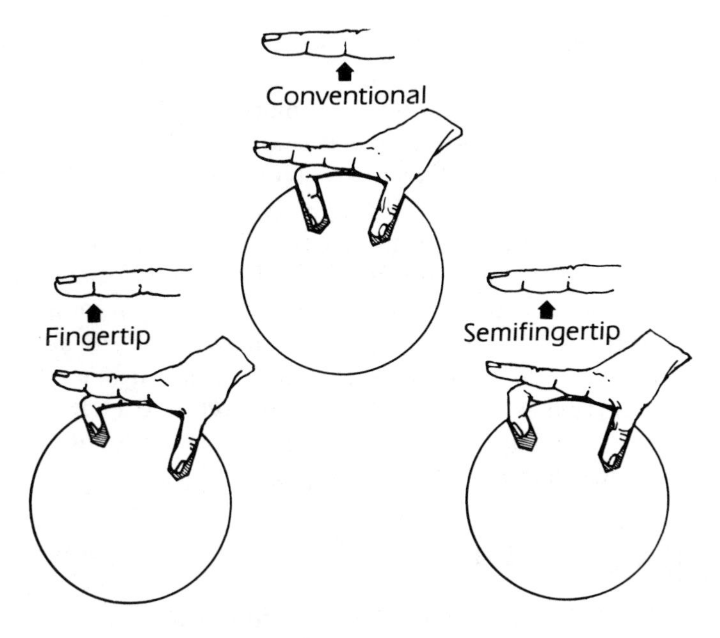

FIGURE 13-3
BASIC GRIPS

Grip

As shown in Figure 13-3, there are three basic grips: conventional, semifingertip, and full-fingertip. You can roll a hook with the conventional grip, but the semifingertip and full-fingertip balls increase the hooking action.

In a conventional grip, the middle and ring fingers are inserted up to about the second knuckle. When you get to be an advanced bowler, you may want to try a semifingertip or full-fingertip grip, as these tend to increase the hooking characteristics of your ball. Considerable strength is needed to master these grips as your fingers are not inserted very far into the ball. For the semifingertip grip, your fingertips are inserted into the finger holes just past the first knuckle. Your fingers go in only to the first knuckle for the full-fingertip grip.

Weighting the Ball

Earlier reference has been made about the effect the overall weight of your ball has on your ability to make strikes. An additional weight factor involves adjusting the weight to the left or right of the ball's center. Adding weight on the right side of the ball, for example, causes the ball to hook more quickly than the conventional ball. This weight adjustment is done by a ball driller with the precise recommendation of a bowling pro who has analyzed your bowling style. The whole process is rather complicated, and you shouldn't attempt to have your ball weighted unless your average is 180 plus for men or 160 plus for women and you have access to a knowledgeable pro.

Starting Position

Here is a final and important note for adjusting your hook ball for both strikes and spares. If on a given day you find your ball is hooking more than usual or less than usual as you roll your pregame warmup balls, don't make any big changes in your technique. Change your starting position instead. Move left, perhaps one board if your ball is hooking more than usual, or move one board right if your ball is hooking less than usual. This is assuming that you are using a precise aiming point as advocated in the spot-bowling section of this book. Keep the same aiming point, but change your starting position to make the necessary adjustment. Remember, this holds true for *both* your strike ball and your spare pickups.

You have control over all the variables listed above except the lane conditions. When you change any one variable, however, it is important to keep everything else constant. Some changes will work well for some bowlers, and others will not. Ask your instructor to help you find which variables work best for you. Consistency and ample rotation as your ball reaches the pocket are your goals.

EXERCISES TO IMPROVE YOUR HOOK BALL

If, with the help of your instructor, you decide to try mastering the full-roller or semiroller, you will need to snap your two middle fingers to your palm as you release the ball. This action increases the spin or rotation on the ball. Considerable strength in your middle fingers is required to do this forcefully, and one way to develop this is to practice lifting your ball from the floor, using only your two middle fingers. Start by lifting the ball five times and build up to thirty lifts. Next, practice rolling the ball on the lanes but hold the ball with just your two middle fingers. To do this, stand just back of the foul line, bend your knees, pick up the ball with two fingers, and swing it back and forth in a pendulum motion, just a few inches off the lane. After a couple of swings, roll the ball down the lane. You will be amazed how much your strength and control increase with this exercise program.

Your index and little fingers also play an important part in making an effective delivery. Remember, a straight wrist is necessary when releasing the ball in order to roll a hook that has good action. Your forefinger and little finger can maintain that straight-wrist position. If you press against the ball with these fingers just before you start your pushaway and maintain that pressure throughout your delivery, you will find that your wrist remains straight.

As you try new and more advanced techniques, your game average can actually drop for a time. But be patient and stick with your new skills. Gradually you will become a better bowler, and your greater sense of accomplishment and personal satisfaction will make all that practice worthwhile.

Appendix

SAMPLE TEST QUESTIONS AND ANSWERS

___ 1. A term used by the English in referring to bowling is (page 4)

A. alonzo
B. kegler
C. skittles
D. poona

___ 2. A religious figure who is prominent in the history of bowling is (page 4)

A. John Calvin
B. Martin Luther
C. John Wesley
D. Mahatma Gandhi

___ 3. The organization which promotes women's bowling is (page 4)

A. WBA
B. WBPA
C. WBO
D. WIBC

___ 4 Which term is synonymous with *cherry*? (page 12)

A. chop
B. blow
C. miss
D. sleeper

___ 5. The thumb position for the hook ball is (page 21)

A. ten o'clock
B. one o'clock
C. nine o'clock
D. twelve o'clock

___ 6. If your thumb is pointing to one o'clock you'll probably throw a (page 21)

A. straight ball
B. hook
C. curve
D. backup

___ 7. For best action as you release the ball, you should (page 78)

A. have fingers come out of holes and then the thumb
B. have thumb come out and then fingers
C. have thumb and fingers come out at the same time
D. turn wrist clockwise with great vigor

___ 8. Dust on the lanes will result in (page 20)

A. less curve on your hook ball
B. fast lanes
C. medium lanes
D. more curve on your hook ball

___ 9. Your first step in the four-step delivery should be (pages 27–28)

A. a long step
B. a quick step
C. a sliding step
D. a short step

___ 10. To increase the action on your ball you should (page 36)

A. release the ball just at the foul line
B. release the ball 15 to 18 inches beyond the foul line
C. release the ball with little, if any, spin
D. release the ball three inches in back of foul line

___ 11. Three strikes in a row is called a (page 14)

A. washout
B. sweep
C. turkey
D. swan

___ 12. A very slow ball is known as a (page 12)

A. leave
B. creeper
C. blow
D. deadball

___ 13. The modern term for the gutter is (page 12)

A. groove
B. side alley
C. trough
D. channel

___ 14. If a bowler is interfered with as he makes his delivery he can (page 64)

A. do nothing about it
B. be given credit for a spare
C. have the ball called "dead"
D. wait and see how many pins fall and then decide whether or not to take the roll over again

___ 15. The 7–10 split is called (page 11)

A. upright
B. goalposts
C. bedposts
D. fieldgoal

___ 16. When you release the bowling ball the first thing it does is (page 22)

A. rolls
B. skids
C. takes
D. spins

___ 17. Most topflight bowlers use (page 23)

A. spot bowling
B. pin bowling
C. natural method
D. target orientation technique

___ 18. The score given a team for an absent member is called (page 11)

A. blind
B. sub-handicap
C. replacement score
D. anchor

___ 19. A bowling term which is synonymous with error is (page 11)

A. goof
B. blow
C. mess-up
D. Jersey

___ 20. The highest score a bowler can make in one frame is (page 54)

A. 20
B. 15
C. 30
D. 10

___ 21. Which of the following spares can be picked up by rolling the strike ball? (page 40)

A. 2–4–7
B. 5–8
C. 1–2–4
D. 3–6–10

___ 22. A hook-ball bowler picks up the 5 pin by (page 42)

A. moving right two boards from strike position
B. rolling ball over third diamond from the right
C. keeping thumb pointed to the right
D. moving left of his or her strike ball position one board

___ 23. To pick up the 1–2–4–7 spare you should (page 42)

A. move one board left of strike position
B. move two boards right of strike position
C. keep thumb pointed to the left
D. roll a strike ball

___ 24. In picking up the 10 pin you should (page 46)

A. roll over the third spot from the right
B. start from the right side of the approach area
C. roll over the second spot from the right
D. roll over the third spot from the left

___ 25. To pick up the 3–6–10 spare you should (pages 46–47)

A. move left of the 10-pin position one board
B. move right of the 10-pin position one board
C. roll ball over second spot
D. roll the ball parallel to the boards

___ 26. The correct position for a straight-ball bowler to pick up the 10 pin is (page 46)

A. four boards from the right side of the lane
B. one board from the left side of the lane
C. three boards from the right side of the lane
D. four boards from the left side of the lane

___ 27. The term a *kegler* is (page 12)

A. a synonym for bowler
B. a type of bowling ball
C. a beginner
D. another name for the pins

___ 28. The 7 pin is picked up by rolling over (page 42)
A. the third spot from the right side of the lane
B. the second spot from the right side of the lane
C. the middle spot

___ 29. The following leave is a baby split (page 11)
A. 3–10
B. 6–10
C. 4–7
D. 1–2

___ 30. A bowler who has no handicap is called a (page 13)
A. classic bowler
B. regular bowler
C. scratch bowler
D. booster bowler

___ 31. If a bowler knocks down six pins on the first ball in the first frame and fouls with the second ball, his score in the first frame is (page 53)
A. 6 plus the second frame
B. 6
C. zero
D. 6 minus the number of pins knocked down with the second ball

___ 32. The most that can be scored in the tenth frame is (page 54)
A. 40
B. 30
C. 50
D. 20

___ 33. The pins left standing after the first ball in a frame are called a (page 13)
A. spare
B. split
C. miss
D. leave

___ 34. A perfect game in bowling is (page 13)
A. 250
B. 400
C. 300
D. 500

___ 35. The purpose of handicaps in bowling is to (page 12)
A. give advantage to the poor bowler
B. give advantage to the good bowler
C. equalize competition
D. make it easier to compute the average

36. List four ways of slowing down the speed of the ball. (page 22)

37. Draw a diagram and number the pins. (page 62)

38. Give two tips in fitting a ball for a person with a conventional grip. (pages 16–17)

39. Score the following games: (pages 55–57)

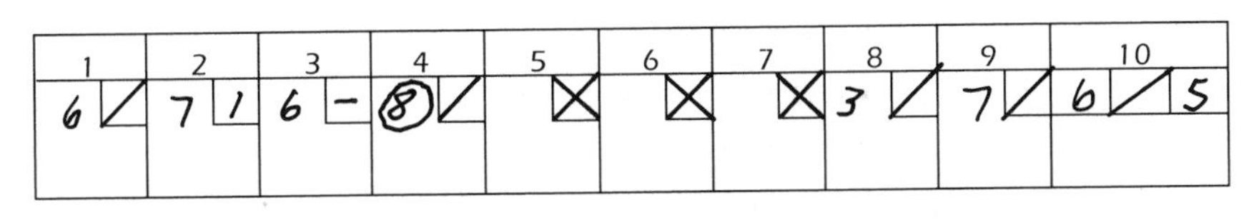

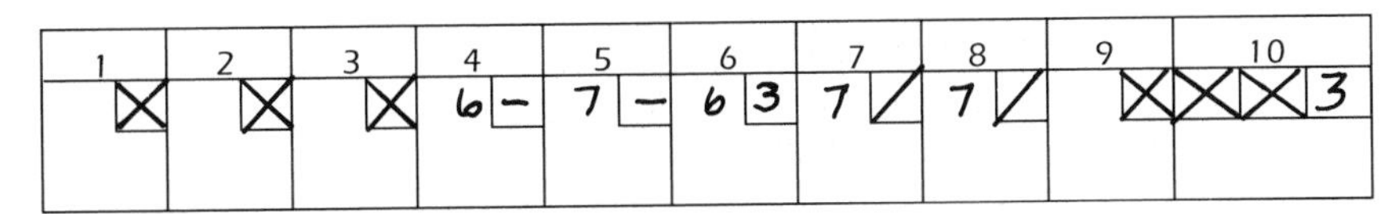

40. Describe three common bowling skill errors or faults and ways of correcting them. (pages 34–36)

ANSWERS TO TEST QUESTIONS

Multiple Choice

1. C
2. B
3. D
4. A
5. A
6. D
7. B
8. D
9. D
10. B
11. C
12. B
13. D
14. C
15. C
16. B
17. A
18. A
19. B
20. C
21. B
22. D
23. B
24. A
25. B
26. D
27. A
28. A
29. A
30. C
31. B
32. B
33. D
34. C
35. C

Short Answer

36. 1. Lower the ball in the starting position.
    2. Shorten your pushaway.
    3. Slow your approach.
    4. Shorten your approach.

37.

7 8 9 10

4 5 6

2 3

1

38. 1. Make sure your thumb will slip in and out of thumbhole easily.
    2. The knuckles of your middle two fingers should be directly over the inside edge of the finger holes.

39.

1	2	3	4	5	6	7	8	9	10
6 /	7 1	6 –	⑧ /	X	X	X	3 /	7 /	6 / 5
17	25	31	51	81	104	124	141	157	172

1	2	3	4	5	6	7	8	9	10
X	X	X	6 –	7 –	6 3	7 /	7 /	X	X X 3
30	56	72	78	85	94	111	131	161	184

40. 1. Error: Pulling arm across the body to your left on the follow-through.

    Correction: Touch your thumb to your right ear on the follow-through and hold for five seconds.

    2. Error: Rushing to the foul line.

    Correction: Make your first step a short one and glide smoothly toward your target.

    3. Error: Twisting your shoulders and losing your balance as you release the ball.

    Correction: Keep your shoulders square to the foul line and "freeze" in that position until your partner taps you on the shoulder.

Index

QUICK REFERENCE SHEET FOR SPOT BOWLING (RIGHT-HANDERS)

Strike Ball, 5–8 Spare, 1–2–5 Spare, 1–2–9 Spare

1. Place your right foot on the dot at the right side of the approach area.
2. Point toes toward 1–3 pocket.
3. Roll ball over the second spot from the right side of the lane. If you roll a hook, your starting position will be three or four boards to the left of the first dot.

Five Pin

1. Line up for strike ball.
2. Roll ball over second spot from the right. Hook-ball bowlers will have to move left one board from the strike position.

Two Pin, 1–2–4–7 Spare, 2–8 Spare

1. Move two boards to the right of your strike position.
2. Roll ball over the second spot from the right into 1–2 pocket.

Ten Pin

1. Place left foot on last board on the left side of the lane.
2. Move four boards to your right.
3. Point toes toward 10 pin.
4. Roll ball over third spot from the right side of the lane. If you roll a hook, start from the last board on the left side of the lane.

Six Pin, 6–10 Spare, 6–9–10 Spare, 3–6–10 Spare, 9–10 Spare, 3–10 Split

1. Move right one board from your position for the 10-pin pickup.
2. Roll ball over third spot from the right side of the lane.

Seven Pin

1. Place your right foot on the last board on the right side of the lane.
2. Move four boards to your left.
3. Point your toes at the 7 pin.
4. Roll ball over third spot from the right side of the lane. If you roll a hook, start eight boards from the right side of the lane.

Four Pin, 4–7 Spare, 4–7–8 Spare, 2–4–7 Spare, 7–8 Spare, 2–7 Split

1. Move left one board from your position for the 7-pin pickup.
2. Roll ball over third spot from the right side of the lane.

QUICK REFERENCE SHEET FOR SPOT BOWLING (LEFT-HANDERS)

Strike Ball, 5–9 Spare, 1–3–5 Spare, 1–3–8 Spare

1. Place your left foot on the dot at the left side of the approach area.
2. Point toes toward 1–2 pocket.
3. Roll ball over the second spot from the left side of the lane. If you roll a hook, your starting position will be three or four boards to the right of the first dot.

Five Pin

1. Line up for strike ball.
2. Roll ball over second spot from the left. Hook-ball bowlers will have to move right one board from the strike position.

Three Pin, 1–3–6–10 Spare, 3–9 Spare

1. Move two boards to the left of your strike position.
2. Roll ball over the second spot from the right into 1–3 pocket.

Ten Pin

1. Place left foot on last board on left side of the lane.
2. Move four boards to your right.
3. Point toes toward 10 pin.
4. Roll ball over third spot from the left side of the lane. If you roll a hook, start eight boards from the left side of the lane.

Six Pin, 6–10 Spare, 6–9–10 Spare, 3–6–10 Spare, 9–10 Spare, 3–10 Split

1. Move right one board from your position for the 10-pin pickup.
2. Roll ball over third spot from the left side of the lane.

Seven Pin

1. Place your right foot on the last board on the right side of the lane.
2. Move four boards to your left.
3. Point your toes toward the 7 pin.
4. Roll ball over third spot from the left side of the lane. If you roll a hook, start from the last board on the right side of the lane.

Four Pin, 4–7 Spare, 4–7–8 Spare, 2–4–7 Spare, 2–7 Split

1. Move left one board from your position for the 7-pin pickup.
2. Roll ball over third spot from the left side of the lane.

BOWLING SKILL ANALYSIS SHEET

	Error	Correction
1. Address Position		
a. Dominant foot back (the opposite midpoint of other foot)		
b. Body erect		
c. Ball held chest high		
d. Little fingers touch—wrist straight		
2. Four-Step Delivery		
a. Short first step—ball extended out and down		
b. Sliding fourth step		
c. Balanced finish		
d. Shoulders square to foul line		
e. Follow-through—hand touches ear		
f. Hand is in correct position in follow through		
g. Left arm is extended sideward for balance		
h. Ball goes over target spot		

Note: This sheet is for the instructor's analysis of each student's performance. It is suggested that the instructor give the students a copy of the analysis and use it as a measure of progress.